Once Upon a V

D-D_ _ _

THE BATTLE FOR EUROPE

by
Dick Bowen and Molly Burkett

ISBN Nº 1 903172 42 X

Published © 2004 Barny Books
Text © Molly Burkett and Dick Bowen
Design © **TUCANN**_design&print_

1944 - 2004

This Book is Number

_268_

Of a first edition of 1000 copies produced to commemorate the 60th Anniversary of
OPERATION OVERLORD

B. L. Montgomery
General

21 ARMY GROUP

PERSONAL MESSAGE
FROM THE C-in-C

To be read out to all Troops

1. The time has come to deal the enemy a terrific blow in Western Europe.

The blow will be struck by the combined sea, land, and air forces of the Allies—together constituting one great Allied team, under the supreme command of General Eisenhower.

2. On the eve of this great adventure I send my best wishes to every soldier in the Allied team.

To us is given the honour of striking a blow for freedom which will live in history; and in the better days that lie ahead men will speak with pride of our doings. We have a great and a righteous cause.

Let us pray that " The Lord Mighty in Battle " will go forth with our armies, and that His special providence will aid us in the struggle.

3. I want every soldier to know that I have complete confidence in the successful outcome of the operations that we are now about to begin.

With stout hearts, and with enthusiasm for the contest, let us go forward to victory.

4. And, as we enter the battle, let us recall the words of a famous soldier spoken many years ago :—

" He either fears his fate too much,
Or his deserts are small,
Who dare not put it to the touch,
To win or lose it all."

5. Good luck to each one of you. And good hunting on the mainland of Europe.

B. L. Montgomery
General
C.-in-C. 21 Army Group.

-6- 1944.

Montgomery's message to his troops - every soldier (in 21st Army group) received a copy

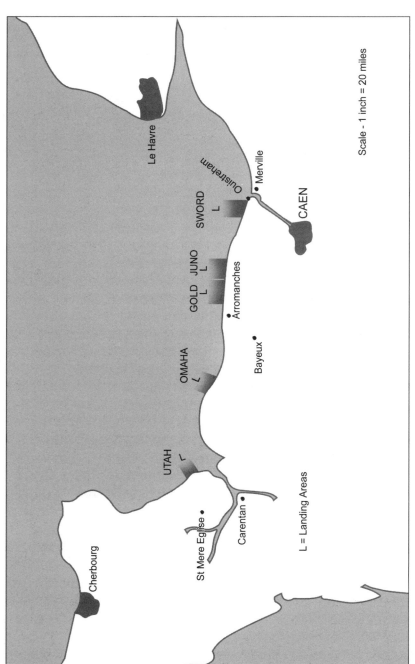

The Invasion Area

Scale - 1 inch = 20 miles

Cherbourg

St Mere Eglise

Carentan

UTAH
L

OMAHA
L

GOLD
L

JUNO
L

SWORD
L

Arromanches

Bayeux

Le Havre

Ouistreham

Merville

CAEN

L = Landing Areas

Operation Overlord
D-Day

Germany invaded Poland in September 1939. This was the start of the Second World War. In the following months German forces invaded Denmark, Norway, Holland, Luxembourg, Belgium and France. During May and June 1940 225,000 Allied troops escaped from France via Dunkirk. Norway was also evacuated during June 1940. This was the month that the French asked the Germans for an Armistice and Italy entered the war.

Britain stood alone in Europe, under threat of invasion. Nevertheless, Churchill's thoughts had already turned towards returning to France although the final decision to invade Western Europe was not taken until the combined meeting of British and American Chiefs of Staff at Washington in May, 1943. General Dwight D. Eisenhower was appointed Supreme Commander-in-Chief Allied Expeditionary Forces of Liberation. Air Chief Marshal Sir Arthur Harris (Bomber Harris) was in charge of Allied Strategic Air Forces with General James Dolittle of the U.S. Eighth Air Force. General Sir Bernard Montgomery was appointed Commander for Assault, Allied Ground Forces. Admiral Sir Bertram Ramsay was appointed Allied Naval Commander in Chief and Air Chief Marshal Sir T. Leigh Mallory was in charge of Allied Expeditionary Air Forces.

Stalin had been urging the allies to start a Western Front to relieve the pressure in the East but the allies were not to be hurried. They would invade when the time was right. Meanwhile thought and ingenuity was the main action. Churchill knew that a harbour was essential. If we didn't have one, then we must make our own and tow it into position. Thus the idea of the Mulberry Harbour was born. The problem of transporting fuel promoted the design and manufacture of Pluto - (Pipe Line under the Ocean). Inventions were welcomed and tested and Hobart's funnies became a reality - Tanks fitted with additions that would enable them to float or lay bridges across ditches or deal with mine fields with flails. Churchill himself submitted several ideas but there are no records that suggest any of them were accepted. Plans were made and tested. No detail was overlooked.

The B.B.C. had appealed for any photographs or post cards that people had obtained when they had visited France. So many poured in that extra staff had to be taken on to sort them out but many of them helped to build up a picture of the suitability of the beaches for the invasion.

Normandy was chosen as the most suitable site for the landings. This was because the area filled the essential requirements. There were sheltered beaches within range of our fighter aircraft with a good road network behind them. They needed calm seas for the landing date, a full moon and low water at first light. June 5th suited all these requirements but a storm blew up in the evening and everything was postponed for twenty four hours.

The war had changed for the Germans. No longer was their Blitzkrieg all successful, instead they were on the defensive protecting their acquisitions rather than on the offensive. Their troops were stretched to the full and they were having to accept youths, old men and foreigners to make up their numbers. They had a long European coast line to guard and were facing defeat in Italy as well as on the Russian front. They knew that the allies were poised to invade but did not know where or when.

Everything was set for D day, June the 6th. 1944.

. . . .

General Dwight D. Eisenhower, Supreme Allied Commander in Chief, Allied Forces of Liberation

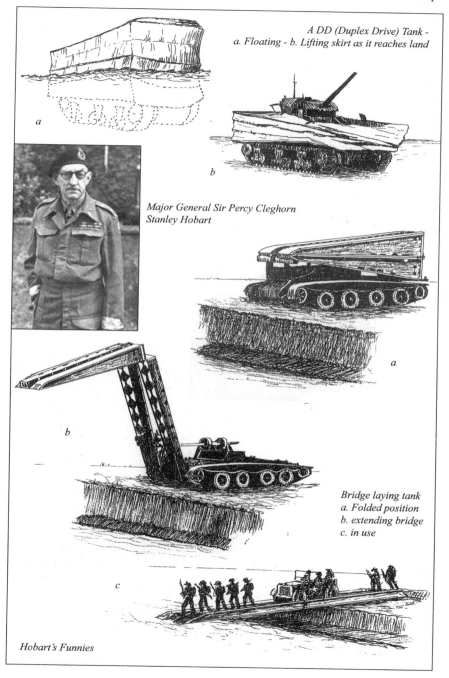

A DD (Duplex Drive) Tank -
a. Floating - b. Lifting skirt as it reaches land

a

b

Major General Sir Percy Cleghorn
Stanley Hobart

a

b

Bridge laying tank
a. Folded position
b. extending bridge
c. in use

c

Hobart's Funnies

7

At Home in England

I lived at Sutton Mandeville. I was an agricultural engineer and had been turned down by the army because I was in a reserved occupation, in other words, I was more use at home. I was over visiting my girl friend at Farnat near Salisbury. We were courting. Jean was packing munitions (bullet belts for the R.A.F.) We used to walk through the countryside and there wasn't a spare inch of ground that was covered by trees that didn't have something stored there, fuel, ammunition, boxes and boxes and crates of the stuff. It was the noise that startled us. It was continuous, a loud roaring noise and the sky filled with aircraft. There were so many that they made the sky dark, every sort of plane, transport aircraft mainly but there were planes towing gliders and fighters. Everybody in the village came out of their houses and were staring up at them. We knew something was going on. It wasn't until the next morning that I heard about D day. All the piles of equipment that had been hidden under the trees had gone as well. Nobody saw it go but it wasn't there any more.

Jean and Ted Mullins.

Commandos preparing for D-Day

W e lived in a children's home at Wyke Regis between Weymouth and Portland. We were on a hill overlooking Portland Harbour. We could see for miles. We had lots of Americans about, They used to pass us in trucks when we were going to and from school and they used to throw sweets and chocolates to us and tins of chocolate and lots of chewing gum. We used to sit at school and dip our fingers in the tinned chocolate powder and suck them. They were billeted all along Chesil Beach, as far as we could see, from Portland to Bridport and up along the Fleet River up to Abbotsbury. Come April there were more and more Yanks coming in. We knew they were Yanks because they had big white stars painted on the sides of the jeeps. There were hundreds of barrage balloons along the coast and searchlights. There were lots of boats in the harbour, all sorts from battleships to fold-up boats that were made with stuff that looked like green tarpaulins. The Americans used to practise in those a lot. Then they all went quiet for a few days. We found out about Slapton Sands• a long time afterwards. There were lots of jeeps lined up in the streets at Weymouth. There just seemed to be more and more of them, nearly all American but some were from Belgium. Then one day we got up and they'd all gone, the boats, the men, the jeeps, everything. There was just one battleship left in the harbour but that evening a ship came in and German P.O.W.s (Prisoners of War) disembarked and were marched up to the prison. They were the first of many. Our patriotism came to the fore then. We boys would stand on the pavement and boo them and sometimes the Germans would threaten us but I don't think they meant it.

Peter and David Neale.

We found out about Slapton Sands a long time afterwards. Slapton Sands was part of a large area of the South Devon Coast taken over for invasion rehearsals by US forces on New Years day 1944, the inhabitants of the local villages having been moved out the previous month. Live ammunition was used during the rehearsals, resulting in some loss of life among the soldiers taking part and damage to many of the properties.

In April 1944 a night exercise was surprised and attacked by a number of German E-boats, which had evaded Royal Navy patrols, and 3 LTCs (tank landing craft) were sunk with the loss of 750 American lives.

Gliders - The First Phase

It was timed to the second. At 00.10 - 00.20 on June 6th. 1944, the Pathfinders went in, their job to mark the landing and dropping zones east of the Orne River for the six gliders that were already approaching their rendezvous. At 00.15. the first British glider landed within fifty yards of the Caen Canal Bridge, its wings snapped off by the tree trunks that had been rammed into the ground and strung with wire.

The metal skids set up sparks as we ran along the ground and then there was a God Almighty crash followed by smashing plywood, dust and a noise like hell and then a sudden silence as we came to a halt. We came to our senses together as we realized we had landed and there was no firing.

D Company of the 2nd Battalion of the Oxfordshire and Buckinghamshire Regiment, (The Ox and Bucks) had landed in France. D Day had begun. In the next thirty minutes, five other gliders carrying the rest of the Battalion had landed.

Gliders at the Orne Bridge

There was no second chance. If we didn't land in the right spot the first time, there wasn't a chance to try a second approach.

I had volunteered to be a glider pilot. There were two conditions we had to fulfil - we had to be fully trained soldiers and we had to pass the R.A.F. aircrew selection tests. I was trained to fly a Horsa at the heavy conversion unit at Brize Norton. The Horsa was a beautifully made machine capable of carrying twenty eight fully armed men. It was 88 feet between the wing tips and was as big as a Dakota. It had been built in furniture factories and was made entirely of laminated plywood sections. There was an overpowering, but not unpleasant smell of new wood and casein glue (made from cows milk). Later on I flew a Hamilcar. That could carry a tank.

I was sent to Tarrant Rushton for special training and was the youngest of the pilots that had been selected. The training was hair raising and hard. We were expected to land our gliders in almost impossible places and to be physically fit. We thought we were being trained for D Day but three days before the mission we found that we were going in the night before. We were shown a sand table with our destination and the terrain surrounding it in every detail, down to the last tree. One thing we did learn and that was that we were landing near Caen. My glider was to be the last of three to land in a specific corner of rough pasture. There was a belt of fifty foot high trees at the end of the field and if I undershot, I would crush my cargo against a fourteen foot high embankment. There was only a few yards on either side for error. It was a daunting enough task in daylight but the landing was to be made in the pitch black of midnight.

It was just before nine o'clock on the evening of June 5th that I walked across the airfield at Tarrant Rushton. The sun was sinking and casting long shadows across the Dorset countryside. I looked at the sky as I suppose all pilots do and watched the light winds sending torn clouds scudding across the sky. I was relieved there was no rain. That could have proved fatal to our mission. I wasn't aware that I was embarking on a feat of navigation which had never been attempted before and I don't believe since. Such was the intensity of our training that I only thought of the job in hand. The success of the operation depended on total surprise and our ability to get the men to the right place at the right time.

My load was waiting for me, twenty eight men of the Ox and Bucks Light Infantry. It was only the second time I had met them. Secrecy had been so tight. The first three gliders were taking off, rumbling on their wheels at the end of the 275 foot tow ropes behind the Halifax Bomber tugs. They were destined for Pegasus Bridge and were to reach this by a longer route but were to land simultaneously with us, a few hundred yards away. We took off at two minute intervals, I was the last of the six to leave, taking off at one minute past 23.00 hours (Double Summer time)..

There was no fear or depression, more a feeling of subdued excitement and a desire to get going.

Our tug gradually turned us away from the sunset. We crossed the coast over Worthing to head south, flying towards a horizon that was pitch black allowing us to adjust our eyes to night vision. We saw no other aircraft, only our tug in front of us at the end of its umbilical line. We even lost sight of that on occasions as we flew through cloud causing a moment or two of worry. The glider pilot must keep his tug in view at all times. Three miles from the French coast, Paddy O'Shea gave us a compass reading confirming that we were on course..

"O.K. You're there," Paddy said. "Go when you like."

We had, in fact, to go at that very moment. Split second timing was essential. I released the tow line. We were on our own, guided through the dark by powerless wings and relying on dead reckoning of the compass and the stopwatch. The roar of the air passing our flimsy craft died to a hiss as we lost speed. The Halifax had released us at 6000 feet so that any watching enemy would think that we were part of a normal bombing raid. From that height, a Horsa would normally glide to earth over twelve miles. Our destination which was only five miles ahead. I had to descend at a really steep angle, 45 degrees, and to slow the craft down sufficiently to prevent overshooting or crash landing. I had to make three changes of course by dead reckoning in exactly six minutes.

Our tug had cast us off at 120 m.p.h.. I immediately applied full

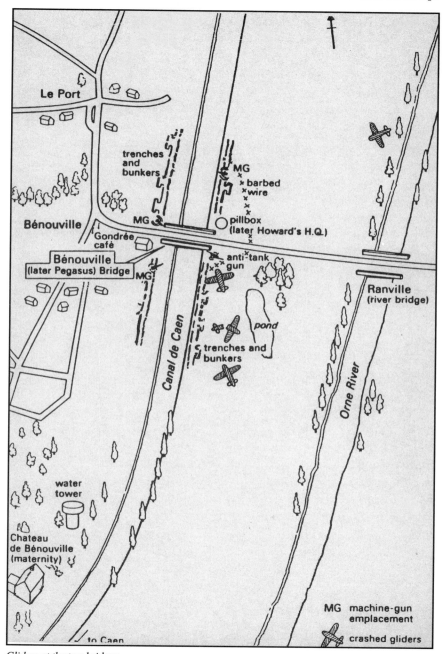

Gliders at the two bridges

flaps to reduce to our planned speed of 80 m.p.h.. Even with the control column pulled hard against my chest, we were nose heavy and I couldn't get her below 90m.p.h.. We were dropping like a brick and I realized at once that we were not only incorrectly loaded, we were overloaded. The men had either brought extra ammunition and grenades on board or, what was much more likely, we had an extra body on board. There were many men that were keen to be in the action. There was no shortage of volunteers. Nobody back at camp had actually mentioned D Day but we all knew.

"Mr Fox," I yelled to the lieutenant in charge, "two men from the front to the back and quickly."

It worked and we were back on course. There was no room for error. Ours was almost a straight descent by the shortest route whereas the three gliders that were aiming for Pegasus Bridge had a gentler and longer descent and the added luxury of circling their landing site before putting down. We were now back on our planned descent rate of 2000 feet per minute. We held our first course of 212 degrees for the allotted 90 seconds. My second pilot, Freddie Baacke, guided us by stop watch lit by the tiniest of hand held lights. We made a turn to 269 degrees which we held for two minutes and thirty seconds. Finally, we turned 212 degrees for the final run in. At our acute angle of descent a standard compass would have been useless and we relied instead on a gyro direction indicator.

As we made our third change of course and were down to 1200 feet, I caught my first glimpse of the Caen Canal and the River Orne running parallel with each other, the waters glistening silver in the moonlight. A rain squall at that moment would have proved fatal. We had no wind screen wipers and no means of aborting the landing. But the whole landscape was just discernible in the diffused light and it looked like the scene that had been laid out on the sand table back at camp. I was afraid that we were still going down too fast and took off the flaps for a few moments to flatten the glide path.

It was a good job I did. I only just missed the top of the fifty foot trees. I immediately employed the parachute brakes, the wheel brakes and full flaps to stop us careering into the embankment at the end of the meadow. There was one final hazard - cows. Nobody had told us that there would be cows grazing in the field. I don't know how I missed them. It was nine minutes after midnight when we came to rest six yards from our allotted spot. There was the briefest moment of silence..

"You're in the right place, Sir," I told Lieutenant Fox and, before I could leave my seat, he and his men had flung open the door and disappeared in a stampede of boots. I was horrified to see that I was the only one of the three gliders to land in the right spot. It looked as though my contingent would have to take the Orne Bridge on their own but the glider that had left immediately in front of me had landed in a field four hundred yards away and the men soon joined up with Mr Fox. The first glider had landed at the wrong bridge altogether because of an error by their tug pilot. The men captured that bridge while they were about it then, with great courage, fought their way to where they should have been.

Roy Howard - Glider Pilot

Roy Howard on his wedding day. He was awarded the Distinguished Flying Medal for his part in the Orne Bridge raid.

Roy Howard

*Glider pilots ready to set out
Roy Howard on right*

Gliders at Canal (now Pegasus) Bridge

W*e were the second of the three gliders that landed alongside the bridge over the River Caen, now called Pegasus Bridge.*

The CO had sent for me on April 23rd and told me that I would be fine flying with Staff Sergeant Barkway. I asked him why and he said that I was an above average pilot navigator and we would be doing some night navigation.

He couldn't have chosen a better man - Geoff Barkway was steady, reliable and unflappable. From then on, we flew together.

We brought our gliders in from 6,000 feet, always landing along the same fence. Then we flew wearing darkened glasses and then we were landing at night. Our eyes grew accustomed to the dark to a certain extent but it was still tricky flying. We crashed three gliders one night. The old timers amongst us knew that something was on.

We were taken to a sealed off area one evening and that was where we met Major John Howard. He was a wonderful man, hard as nails but the sort that gives you confidence. By the time we left we knew exactly what was expected of us. We had to land our cargo of men, then carry guns and ammunition to the bridge. A model of the area where we were to land was on a table and Major Howard pointed to the landing grounds. The model was so detailed that it even had glass in the windows.

We had practised so often that it all seemed familiar, except that we had men on board rather than blocks of concrete. We crossed the English Coast at Worthing and touched the French Coast at Cabourg. The Halifax navigator announced we were on target. He gave us the wind speed and direction.

"OK you've got it, go when you like."

Geoff pulled the toggle and we were on our own.

I had a small battery in a case strapped to the underside of my wrist and a tiny light in the palm of my hand which gave just enough light to read the map.

Geoff pulled the glider a bit to give us some more height but we were overweight and only lifted about fifty feet.

Peter Boyle

Geoff sat on the right of the glider and myself on the left, in reverse to the usual seating because Geoff needed to make two sharp right turns. We knew the route we had to take, the wind speed, the direction. We turned right soon after crossing the coast, then right again but I didn't need to give Geoff any more directions; the moon was showing through a gap in the clouds and we could see that the first glider had landed in front of us.

Everything seemed to be going to plan until we hit water. Everything happened at once. The cockpit broke away from the main body and rolled over and I was caught in the debris. I was stunned for a second or two but came to as Geoff was shouting and clearing the shattered wood to pull me free.

The Medical Officer who had been on our glider was badly concussed and did not seem to know where he was. A body was caught in the main spar, but the rest of the men had already vacated the glider. I had lost my helmet and all my equipment but there wasn't time to worry about that. There was shouting and shooting from the bridge.

I fetched the PIAT from the glider and ran with it to the bridge. I told someone I had it and he said, "One's no good without the other."

A PIAT is an anti tank missile and it's heavy. One man holds it over his shoulder and another loads it with a bomb and fires it.

I ran back to fetch the ammunition but not before I'd seen the medical officer wandering across the bridge. He didn't know where he was. John Howard turned him round and he wandered back again. As I ran back I heard Geoff shouting that he had been shot and I ran across to him. His hand was almost hanging off at the wrist and he was losing a lot of blood. It was the blood that brought the medical officer back to sensibility. Geoff was treated. Men arrived with a stretcher and he was carried to the First Aid post that was being set up.

> I could remember taking the glider in and pulling Peter out of the debris and I don't remember another thing, not until I came to on the beach lying on the sand along with other wounded men.
>
> We were taken off on a landing craft. I finished up at the hospital in Leeds. There wasn't anti-biotics in those days and gangrene had set in, I lost my arm, taken off at the shoulder.
>
> I was eventually fitted with a false arm and invalided out in 1947.
>
> **Staff Sergeant Geoff Barkway - Glider Pilot**

Geoff Barkway

I carried the ammunition back to the bridge just as a machine gun started firing from a point on the far bank. Major Howard shouted at us to take it out and I found myself part of a fighting unit. There was a lull for a short while; then the Germans attacked from the far side but we held the bridge. A PIAT took out the leading German tank and the flames lit up the area. Reinforcement paras and equipment came in *about this time and we needed them. Fighting was fierce but every man knew what he had to do. About seven o'clock the bombardment started from the sea and the noise was in the background. My whole memory is of noise, gunfire, shouting and explosions.*

Then, at mid-day, there was this noise which we couldn't identify. One of the men said, "It's bagpipes," and there's this piper leading Lord Lovat and his long line of commandos along the road - one thousand of them. We couldn't believe it. There was his lordship with his walking stick and a couple of commandos behind him pushing a pram and others spread out in a long line behind them.

Peter Boyle

I got my head down for a bit then. We had been ordered to return on June 8th. I went with Guthrie and Pearson. Some of the glider pilots had already gone. The beachmaster told us to wait beneath the wall and we were joined by two glider pilots from the Merville Battery. We were taken off at 16.00 hours by landing craft.

I reported back. They were short of glider pilots and I thought I would be needed, but I wasn't. I was given a replacement uniform and three days leave. I felt real smart in my new gaiters and boots. I walked up the hill at Radcliffe and there was my Godmother. She and the headmaster's wife had the biggest voices in Nottingham.

"Thought you'd have been out there fighting with the others," she shouted out.

"I've just come back," I said and never spoke to her again.

Staff Sergeant Peter Boyle - Glider Pilot

The Horsa Gliders which landed at Pegasus Bridge.

As soon as the first glider had landed, Major John Howard was out of the door rallying his men, shouting, "Up the Ox and Bucks. Up the Ox and Bucks." He was quickly joined by the other two platoons. They achieved complete surprise.

They came out of the night. I was on guard duty on the bridge. I was seventeen years old and three weeks. I'd been a member of the Hitler Youth and was proud to belong to it. I was proud to volunteer for the army but it hadn't been exciting. Nothing happened. We'd been told to look out for paratroops but we'd been told that so often that it had become a bit of a joke. Then they were there and we hadn't heard them coming. I ran. I don't mind admitting it. I was scared to death. I shouted to the other guard to run but he drew his gun and started shooting. I kept running and went along the bank and hid there. We stayed there for two days. Some of the others came and joined me When it grew quiet, we went back with our hands up to surrender but they didn't want us and sent us back along the bank.

Private Helmut Romer - German soldier

....

The men swarmed over the bridge, silencing the pill boxes with grenades thrown through the slits. The German N.C.O.s fought until they were killed. Their men fled. The Ox and Bucks had taken the bridge in ten minutes. The rest of Howard's force seized the other bridge in a similar time. Major Howard put his defence in order. The Germans were already organizing a counter attack in Benouville, a village to the west of the bridge. The bridge had to be held until reinforcements arrived from the 5th Parachute Brigade of the 6th Division.

On the far side of the bridge was a small café called Café Gondrée. Mme Arlette Gondrée tells of how the family sheltered in the cellar until there was a knock on the door and her father answered it to find Major John Howard waiting there. He had come to introduce himself and his troops. It was the first of many meetings. The café is still there and has been renamed after the men who recaptured the bridge. The men of the Airborne troops wore the insignia of Pegasus, the winged horse of Bellerophon. The bridge has been renamed the Pegasus Bridge and the café is known as The Pegasus Café.

The 6th Airborne Division went in at Area Sword which was mainly to

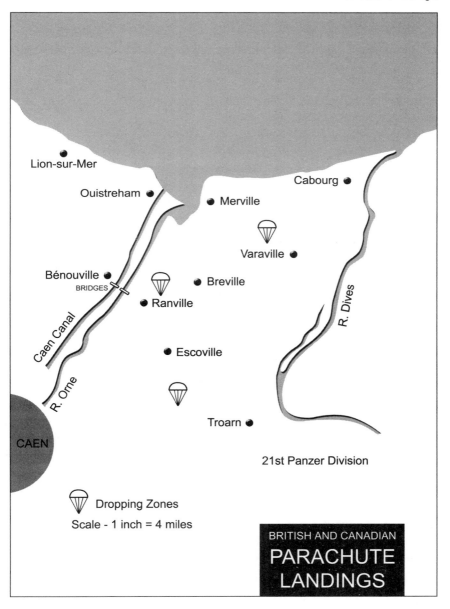

Lion-sur-Mer

Cabourg

Ouistreham

Merville

Varaville

Bénouville

BRIDGES

Breville

Ranville

Caen Canal

R. Dives

Escoville

R. Orne

CAEN

Troarn

21st Panzer Division

Dropping Zones

Scale - 1 inch = 4 miles

BRITISH AND CANADIAN

PARACHUTE
LANDINGS

the east of Sword Beach and included the River Orne and the Canal de Caen and the two main bridges over them. The area had to be secured during the night of D day to allow the troops landing on the beaches space to advance. Three brigades landed, two of parachute troops and one of gliderborne.

The 1st and 2nd Glider Pilot Wings of The Glider Pilot Regiment were attached to the Sixth Airborne Division.

Field Marshal Gerd von Rundstedt was Commander of German forces in the west. He commanded sixty divisions, eleven of them armoured, ready to face the allied invasion threat. These were held from the Dutch coast round to the Spanish border. One division was stationed on the Channel Islands and another on the Mediterranean coast in case the allies invaded from North Africa or Italy. The Germans did not know where the allies were likely to invade.

General Dwight D.Eisenhower, The Supreme Commander of the Allied Forces, had 37 Divisions and it would take at least seven weeks before they could all be landed. He faced two problems, how to keep the Germans widely spread out, to keep them guessing about the likely invasion point and to prevent them moving quickly to the invasion beaches once the first landing had been made.

Operation Taxable was set up to mislead the Germans into thinking the invasion was to be in the Pas de Calais region. The dummy landings from the south east coast were coded Operation Fortitude. Operation Overlord was the name given to the genuine landings. Dummy landing craft, dummy piers, dummy gliders were placed in the eastern and south eastern counties of the UK to suggest landings were likely to be made towards the French-Belgian borders. The R.A.F. bombed as many communication points as possible, making sure they dropped bombs further east as well.

The French underground movement was active in the destruction, blowing up railway lines and junctions as well as other targets. The R.A.F. dropped thousands of weapons to the underground. As soon as they received the coded messages via the B.B.C. that the invasion was to take place, they increased their activities throughout Normandy adding to the chaos amongst the Germans.

The German officers could only agree on one thing and that was that the invasion was coming. Field Marshal Erwin Rommel and most of his officers were sure it would take place in the Pas de Calais region although they were suspicious of the activity to the west but saw it as a diversion to the real invasion. Hitler who had put Rommel in charge of the troops guarding the coast from Holland to the Loire had decided that the invasion would take place between Cherbourg and Le Havre but his Generals did not agree. Runstedt's advisers had assured him that the Normandy coast was too rocky for a landing and the flooding round the mouth of the River Vire would limit any threat to the Cotentin Peninsula. They did strengthen the Atlantic wall, the almost impenetrable coastal defences that were built along the French and Channel Island coasts These strong points were so strong, that the remnants of many of them can still be seen today. Rommel designed many of these additional deterrents himself - sharply pointed stakes that would pierce the bottoms of shallow assault boats, others with mines fastened to them, concrete and wire triangles, blocks of all sizes and shapes and thousands of mines and booby traps.

The Germans were sure that something was going to happen. Rommel was convinced that the invasion would be at high tide and when the weather conditions were right. He had expected the allies to land in May but when May had passed and they had not moved, he was sure that there would be no invasion until the end of June.

The R.A.F. had been flying almost continuous sorties, bombing sites of prime importance, particularly the German radar sites. Although they bombed along the Normandy coast, most of their activities were in the Pas de Calais region purely to mislead the Germans. On the night of 5th/6th June the planes dropped window strips (metallic paper) over the Channel which showed up on the radar. Small boats were sent out towing balloons which showed up on the screen as large ships. It was so successful that German fighters spent four hours searching for this non existent fleet while the gliders crossed the coast further south carrying members of the Ox and Bucks towards the River Orne. Obviously the Germans were expecting something big. The jamming of their radar and the reports from the Pas de Calais area was enough to cause concern. There was also a big increase of B.B.C. activity that evening giving coded messages to the French Resistance leaders who had key targets such as railways and telephone lines to sabotage. Some of them had been betrayed and the Germans lay in wait for them. All the same, Rommel was convinced this was a trick. The weather on the night of the 4th - 5th was too bad to attempt a landing. There had been a storm the previous night and the sea was too rough to attempt a crossing. In any case, it would be a low tide in the morning. He took the opportunity to go home to Germany and visit his wife.

Briefing 6th Airborne

By 2 a.m. the parachutists had landed. The first had been jumping as the Ox and Bucks were taking the bridges. These men were the elite - tough men who had been training for months for their role. Their tasks were three fold, - to support the men holding the two bridges over the Orne and the canal, (It was essential that these were held as this was the route that German supplies and reinforcement would take to reach the beaches.) - to destroy the five bridges across the River Vire to prevent counter attacks from the Germans, and the 9th Battalion was to destroy the guns in the heavily fortified Merville Battery. This was considered the most important task. The Merville Battery overlooked Sword beach on which the troops were going to land. It had to be put out of action.

They'd dropped the flares to guide the Dakotas in. German searchlights were sweeping the sky. The whole scene was lit up and then we saw the circles of white gliding down towards us and we knew the paras were on their way. We were going to be OK.
Soldier from Ox & Bucks

I landed in the middle of Pegasus Bridge and I knew I shouldn't be there. A battle was raging, I didn't hang about. I collected my kit and ran to where I should have been - Ranville. Things weren't much better there.
Jock from Bradford

The 7th Battalion of the Parachute regiment's 5th brigade rushed to rescue the Ox and Bucks landing to the east of the two bridges.

We landed right in the middle of it. The wind was pretty strong and we got blown all over the place. A bloke that landed near me had been shot on the way down and he wasn't the only one. I had to leave him. My job was to get to the bridge and I'd hardly disentangled myself from the parachute than the bugler was blowing his bugle and we knew it was for us. We'd heard it often enough to know our own regimental call but we could see where we were going. There was one terrific explosion followed by the sound of exploding ammunition and we could see the bridge and the silhouettes of the men against the flames of a burning tank. They needed our help and we ran.

The Germans had counter attacked. John Howard's troops had destroyed the lead tank and it was this explosion that had alerted the paras. The 7th Battalion attacked and cleared the Germans out of Benouville but General Richter's 716th Division counter attacked again and again with tanks and infantry. "A" Company was almost wiped out but they held the town even though they had lost all their officers.

Fighting on the other side of the bridges was equally fierce. Ranville was the target for the 12th (Yorkshire) Parachute Battalion and they literally fought to the death. The officers were either killed or wounded and the men were led by their NCOs. Sergeants Jones and Millburn were awarded Distinguished Conduct Medals for their leadership at Ranville. They were both killed later in the campaign.

Many of the parachutists had failed to land in the right areas. The Dakota pilots had changed course to avoid the heavy flak and were unable to identify landmarks. The wind was stronger than they had expected and many were blown off course.

I jumped when the green light came on but, as I left the plane, my head hit the side and my helmet was knocked off. I was lost without it. My map and instructions were all in my helmet. It's a peculiar experience jumping in the dark because you can't see the falling ground until you hit it and I hit it hard. I unclipped my chute and shoved it under a hedge and started looking round for the others but there was no one there. It was dark and silent. I walked along a lane for a while hoping to meet up with my mates but there was nothing and no one. I would have to wait for daylight. I clambered over a wall and fell down six feet or so. The road was above the field. I threw my kit into a patch of nettles and settled down with my back against the wall to wait. I could have done with a cigarette but that was the last thing I could do. There's nothing like cigarette smoke for giving your position away. It travels along the ground for up to a hundred yards and British cigarettes have a different smell to the German ones. I must have dozed off because the next thing I remember was a gun being put to the back of my head and a cockney voice saying, "Do you want to buy a submarine?" there were three parachutists with their blackened faces grinning down at me. They were making their way to the Merville Battery and suggested I went with them. They were already walking on across the field, below the wall as they said this. I didn't need a second invitation. I was in a hurry to keep them in sight and catch up with them. I dived into the nettles for my kit and, at that second, a machine gun started up and the three men fell, one after the other. I dropped to the ground face down in the nettles and waited for the gun to fire at me but nothing happened. The two German soldiers couldn't have seen me. Perhaps I was bending down for my kit at the moment they had seen the others. I lay there and waited for them to move on but they weren't in any hurry. They sat on the wall chatting and smoking. I wanted to move more into the nettles. They were sure to see me if they came to look at the men they had killed but they didn't seem concerned about them. They eventually went off. I gathered myself together and collected a map from one of the men I had met earlier on. At least I had some sense of direction now. I made my way cautiously towards the river when I was stopped by another para pointing his gun at me. He demanded my identification, password and so on. It was obvious I was English but he still went on with his questions. Then he called out to the men in the field behind him, "Philip, your brother's here."

He was fastening his boots. He looked up and said, "Hello kid." It was the first time that I'd seen him since I joined up.

Parachutist of 7th Battalion

Gliders and tugs leaving for Normandy

On the way

The bugle rallying call had only collected 200 men out of an expected force of 620 by two a.m. The sound of heavy firing from the direction of Benouville made them move, hoping that the stragglers would find their own way which many of them did. Meanwhile other troops were already at work, clearing Rommel's asparagus (the posts he had erected to make landing from the air difficult) and preparing the ground where the 69 gliders carrying the brigade's heavier equipment were due to land at 03.00 hours.. These weapons were essential if the bridges were to be held.. As it was, most of the gliders crash landed because there had not been enough men to prepare the ground in time.. Men set to, to cut the guns and vehicles free. By first light, the brigade was dug in on both sides of the bridges and ten anti tank guns were being moved into position.

General Richard Gale (Windy Gale) came in on a glider at this time. His other unit, the 9th Battalion was experiencing extreme difficulties in achieving their task, the destruction of the Merville Battery. This covered 35 acres and was situated one mile from the village of Merville overlooking the beaches on which the British and Canadians would be landing. The sea side resort of Home sur Mer lies to the east and to the west is the low land where the River Orne and the Caen Canal reach the sea. The guns of the Battery could have wreaked havoc on the invading forces. They had to be destroyed. The Battalion's Commanding Officer, Lt. Colonel Terence Otway, of The Royal Ulster Rifles, had landed with his party beside a German Battalion Headquarters and had difficulties reaching the rendezvous. He discovered only a fragment of his men had found their way and there were hardly any weapons or special equipment. He waited for nearly two hours for stragglers to arrive but decided he could wait no longer. He had 150 men. By this time the area was full of Germans on the alert. Resourcefulness, courage and improvisation won the day. Major George Smith and some of the Paras had reached the rendezvous on time.. They had found a way through the barbed wire and the minefield. They did not have the tape to mark the path so they had kicked up a line of turf that needed to be followed.

Five gliders that should have brought essential equipment failed to arrive. Only fifteen men of the breaching group had reached the rendezvous, many had landed in the wrong place, troops and supplies were widely scattered. Otway wasted no time in organizing the men in his command. He divided the breaching groups into teams under the command of Major Alan Parry.. They were to breach the wire in two places throwing themselves over the wire to protect the attacking troops who clambered over their backs. The men were protected by their thick uniforms and the packs they carried. Speed and surprise was essential but the men still had minefields to cross. The whole area was covered with machine gun nests and heavy fire power. Every inch of the way was protected. The assault group had been divided into four teams, each one responsible for destroying a gun emplacement. A diversionary party was to attack the main gate.

They went in at 04.00 hours.

All hell broke out. We had had weeks of training but nothing had prepared us for this. The second the signal was given, we were running and we were in. We knew what we had to do. Everyone was shouting, "Get in, get in, get in," Lieutenant Twinkletoes Jefferson was blowing his hunting horn and running. He was a big man and, although it was dark, I could see his shape and I kept up with him. It wasn't easy. The bombers had bombed this area and we had to avoid bomb craters and it was still dark. Some of the men trod on mines and were blown up but we kept going. We knew what was expected of us and we couldn't hesitate or think of anything else. You felt strangely alone out there but you knew the others were near you. The phosphorescent glow of recognition tags, the skull and cross bones moved through the night.. Our men were still shouting and the German machine guns were firing. Beams of light flashed across the scene and everywhere was the smell of cordite and dust. Then the hunting horn stopped and we knew that the Lieutenant had been hurt. Five of us made it to the gun emplacement and we sheltered against the wall for a few seconds, out of range of the bullets. The whole area was being covered by machine gun fire. We leaned against the wall to get our breath and I, for one, wondered how we had crossed the area unscathed. We dropped grenades down the air vent. There was a terrific explosion, then screams, then silence. The sergeant put up his hand to keep us quiet and we could hear voices along the passage so we tossed in more grenades. The whole area was full of smoke and dust. The sergeant called out the only German word he knew,

"Kamerade, kamerade,(friend), " and these Germans started staggering out. There were about twenty of them and we didn't know what to do with them. They were pitiful. Some of them knelt down and pleaded with us not to shoot them. Others kept repeating "Kamerade," We took their guns and lined them up, then we went in and dealt with the gun.

N.C.O. 9th Battalion - Parachute Regiment

L t Col. Otway lost many of his men. He withdrew with those that were left and had the satisfaction of signalling the success of the operation with a quarter of an hour to spare. One of the men had a yellow flare and that was their only means of signalling. He just hoped the captain of the Arethusa, a cruiser of the Bombardment Force D, would understand. The other officers were keen to move out. If the message had not been understood, the Arethusa would open fire at 05.50 hours. They were anxious to get the survivors out before then. The medics stayed behind and fixed up a centre to deal with the wounded in a barn along the road. A German medic stood guard in the doorway and, although there was plenty of German activity, none of them bothered the wounded men.

Men had landed in treetops or in flooded areas and had had to dump all their kit to save themselves but groups of stragglers continued to trickle in to their battalion areas even as they were lining up to move on. Their orders were to advance some three miles to Le Plein and hold on to the village at all costs. There was a footbridge over the river and that had to be kept safe until the commandos arrived to relieve them.

We moved out at 08.30 hours. There were Germans everywhere but they weren't organized. They didn't seem to understand what was happening to them. We moved fast but cautiously. The Colonel divided us into groups to crawl across a field of growing corn. Thinking we couldn't be seen, we took a short rest which gave us a chance to gather our thoughts and our strength. The French were incredible. They were carrying on their every day life as if this drama wasn't going on around them. They obviously knew we were there but ignored us except for one farmer who waded through the corn and insisted on shaking hands with the Colonel. He then went on to discuss the weather and the state of the crops and there was the Colonel trying to be polite and wishing him out of the way. When the Colonel told him that it was his men that had taken Merville Battery, there was no slowing down our new friend's enthusiasm. He started wading through the corn trying to shake our hands. A similar thing happened a mile further on when we were sheltering in ditches. This time the man was more helpful. He told the Colonel that the Germans and some Russian P.O.W.s were entrenched at Hauger which joined Le Plein so we managed to avoid them and get to our rendezvous. The Colonel took over a building as his H.Q. but it wasn't long before the Germans realized where we were and attacked. We held them off but we lost more men and started to run low on ammunition. Even in those conditions the unbelievable happened. Sergeant Bedford had been separated from his mate and asked everybody if they had seen him but you don't look for other people when you're in battle. He was sure his pal had been killed when, just as the guard was changing, this voice could be heard calling, "Eric, Eric."

"That's Tich," the Sergeant said and started shouting out his name and Tich came wandering over as if he was out for a walk on a Sunday afternoon and the pals were together again.

....

It was getting too dangerous in the building and the Colonel moved us out. Our group was sheltering in a ditch. The first we knew that the Commandos had arrived was when they attacked the house with the big wall where the Germans were sheltering. I hadn't seen them come over the bridge and I don't think anyone else had either. The Colonel took a couple of men with him towards the bridge to meet the main group. It was a glorious day. The storm of the previous day had blown itself out. We heard the bagpipes first and there was Brigadier the Lord Lovat walking over the bridge, carrying a swagger stick, his revolver in its holster, accompanied by his piper. Everything about the two men was smart and shining. The Colonel shouted out that one of the Commando units was having a sticky time and he wasn't going out there to meet him. At that point a mortar shell whizzed over our heads and landed near his Lordship who must have decided that Otway's position was safer and joined him in the ditch. The Commandos strengthened the assault and the Germans began to withdraw. We returned to the chateau and waited for the Commandos to relieve us.

NCO 9th Battalion - Parachute Regiment

Men of the 9th Battalion also managed to destroy the five bridges over the River Vire, preventing any counter attacks from the Germans.

The 8th Parachute Battalion and the 1st Canadian Parachute Battalion destroyed the bridges over the Dives. The most important was the bridge near Troarn. A major and five sappers destroyed this in great style. Their glider had landed them and their jeep miles away but they managed to find their way through the woods and drove through Troarn at top speed with their sten guns blazing. They blew the bridge, dumped the jeep and made their way to their Battalion on foot.

Brigadier Lord Lovat and his men fought their way to the bridges over the Orne and Caen Canal. He had bet John Howard that he would be there for twelve o'clock but he lost his bet. He arrived at ten past. The Paras heard the bagpipes playing and then they saw his Lordship looking as smart as a new pin marching towards them as if he did not have a care in the world.

At 00.20 hours, the American pathfinders landed in France. Those for the 101st Airborne lit the way with their homing beacons but those of the 82nd Airborne had landed amongst German troops and had not been able to mark the landing fields.

00.30. - 1,056 R.A.F. bombers bombed the coastal batteries that covered the invasion beaches.

We flew out of Binbrook.. We were briefed as usual and we had our targets. There was the usual amount of flak but we dropped our bombs and made for home. It was a normal raid for us. It wasn't until later that morning that we learned it was D day and our raids had signalled the start of it.

Squadron Leader, Charles Wearmouth DFC

....

They had to time their flights to the minute and be out of the way for the huge air fleet that was carrying the first of the invasion forces, 850 transport planes carrying the American 82nd and 101st Airborne Divisions and 260 carrying the British 6th and 9th Airborne Divisions to their drop zones. They were followed by hundreds more transport planes towing gliders filled with more soldiers and essential equipment. These'men were the elite amongst the fighting forces and all of them were volunteers.

We took off from Lyneham. It was a beautiful evening and we sat on the grass beside the runway waiting for the order to move. I suppose we were all a bit quiet wondering what was in front of us. The padre had the idea that we should have a sing song and one of the ground crew was sent to get the piano. I played a few tunes and everyone seemed to be singing, even the air crew. Then it was time to go.

....

The planes carrying the American troops ran into trouble as they approached the French coast. The clouds were low and the flak fierce. Many of the pilots were inexperienced. It was dark and they were lost. Then one of the planes was hit and blew up in a huge orange ball of flame and the others scattered., dropping their sticks of parachutists wherever they thought it was safe. It was particularly difficult for the pilots carrying the 82nd for there were no markers to guide them. Many of the men were dropped in the wrong place.

Major General Ridgeway's troops, the 82nd, were to take the area between the Utah beach and the German reserves, to capture and hold St Mere Eglise which was on the road from Cherbourg, the likely route for German reinforcements, and to take bridges that crossed the River Merderet. One Regiment, the 505th,,was to drop to the north east of St.Mere Eglise, take the town and set up a road block across the Cherbourg road.

The 101st (The Screaming Eagles) under Major General Maxwell Taylor's command was to land between the 82nd (The All Americans) and the coast and open up the exits from the beaches and to block any German counter attacks by capturing Carentan, three miles west of the River Vire.

The red light turned green and the call went up - Get out, get out, get out and as I pulled the rip cord I was floating down into the unknown. We knew there were poles in the fields below us so I lowered my kit bag which was suspended on a forty foot rope from my harness. It landed and I felt the jolt, then I hit the ground and rolled on to my back. I didn't know where I was. Hundreds and hundreds of parachutes and containers were coming down. The sky was a picture of light and flak. Then a plane exploded sprinkling thousands of burning pieces across the sky.

Both divisions were widely scattered, particularly the 82nd. They had expected to land to the west of the River Merderet. Instead they landed astride it. Only four per cent landed in the right place.

The Germans had flooded the area and the river valley was marshy and covered with water. Two Regiments landed in this flooded area and 36 of the men weighed down by their heavy packs were drowned. American troops carried up to 80 rounds of rifle ammunition, rations, water and spare clothing in their packs as well as other essential equipment needed for their role in the battle ahead. Army issue boots were heavy and difficult to remove quickly for those men that landed in the water.

I landed in water and started to sink. It covered my head and I had to jump to get some air. I was weighed down by the equipment strapped to my leg and I couldn't kick it off. I started to panic but my brain was telling me to think rationally and that isn't easy when you have to keep jumping to get a breath of air. I got my knife and tried to cut through the straps that fastened the kit but it wasn't any good. I thought I would drown. Then common sense prevailed and I looked at the knife. I was cutting with the blunt side. I sliced through the strap quickly enough then and waded to the shallow water and met up with my mate who was wading towards the higher ground. Was I pleased to get on dry land.

1,100 of Taylor's paratroopers, the Screaming Eagles, reached the rendezvous by dawn. They should have numbered 6,000. The 82nd's 505th Regiment assembled its 2nd and 3rd Battalions on the outskirts of St Mere Eglise.. Rather than land where they had expected, thirty of them landed in the town itself. The R.A.F. had bombed a building in the market square and the Mayor had broken curfew to line up people passing buckets of water to put out the flames. The Germans had turned out to guard the locals. It was into this scene that the first American dropped. Nobody took any notice of him. He unfastened his parachute and walked round the back of the buildings. Others that followed him weren't so fortunate.

It was a turkey shoot. The whole area was lit up by the flames from a burning building and we were aiming straight for the town square and the Church bells were ringing. All I could think was what I was going to do to that Goddam pilot when I met up with him again. I swung my legs to try and get to one side. I was lucky, I landed down a little street and I didn't waste any time getting out of there but I had time to see that some of the men lay where they fell. The Jerries had shot them out of the sky and there was one man caught up in a tree and calling for help but there was nothing I could do. Then there was this dreadful scream as a para landed in the middle of the burning building. The screams didn't last long but for those few seconds, the whole of the scene in the market square seemed to freeze. It was all those years ago but I still see that scene in my mind. I still dream about it.

Soldier of the 505th Regt.

A problem was the actual parachute release methods. The British had a quick release mechanism. The Americans had to unfasten their belts and it took too long in some cases. One man was caught by his rigging on the steeple of the Church and hung there for several hours before he was released. Survivors made their way out of the town in the darkness. Lieutenant Colonel Krause' 3/505th had landed within a mile of the town. 90 men assembled there. The officer got hold of a drunk Frenchman and used him as a guide to get to St Mere Eglise.

Lt. Col. Krause

The Americans had different parachutes to other Allied troops. They had to pull a rip-cord to release the chute when they left the plane. Those of the British troops were connected to a cable which was joined to a fixed point in the plane. The cable would pull the parachute as the soldier left the plane causing it to open automatically. The Americans also carried an Emergency Chute. The British did not.

The Americans carried "crickets," small clickers with which they could identify comrades in the dark. Some German groups realized their significance and made a similar noise to draw the Americans towards them. Then they shot them.

I got out of that town double quick and it was real dark away from that blaze in the square. I didn't know where I was but wherever it was, I knew I shouldn't be there. Well, I got this cricket and I clicked it and there was an answer straight away and there was this other guy right behind me. We could have touched each other, well almost. It was that dark, we couldn't see each other. We didn't think anyone else would see us either, but as we went by one cottage, a voice came out of the darkness and said, "Bonjour."

And, as we passed other houses, there would be similar greetings.

We got to the main road and started walking east, towards the rendezvous. It was real dark and quiet. We clicked our crickets from time to time and there were ten or eleven of us before we'd gone a mile. We hadn't gone much further before we realized something was going on up front. It was a sort of rustling, a regular kind of sound. When you were in a situation like we were, you develop a sixth sense. We made for the hedges at the side of the road. Whether it was because our eyes were becoming used to the dark or whether it was that the sky was beginning to lighten, I don't know but we were able to identify this group of people coming in our direction. They were weaving a bit from one side of the road to the other. And as they came abreast of us, we saw they were our own men. There was a local in front of them and he seemed very drunk and very happy and behind him was the Colonel with his pistol pushed into the Frenchman's back. Nobody was going to argue with a man like that and the Frenchman didn't try. Everything about the Colonel was menacing. He meant business. I clicked my cricket. I didn't want them to think I was a Nazi and shoot me. The Colonel didn't even look in my direction. "You're late," he said, "get fell in."

We marched right back to St Mere Eglise, right into the market square. They got our men out of the trees and the poor devil off the Church tower as well as a German sniper who had been hiding in the Church and could have shot the rookie at any time but he was frightened to do that in case anyone realized he was there and shot him. We marched right on to the German barracks behind the drunk Frenchman. The German soldiers had gone back to bed. We soon tipped them out of there. Eleven who resisted were shot. We took the weapons off the others and sent them out of town. The Colonel didn't stop to draw breath. HQ was to be set up in an orchard which had been marked on his map. Fifty of us were detailed to set up a road block to the west of the town. We soon got dug in there. Later that morning, two of the Germans we'd turned out of the barracks tried to surrender to us. We couldn't do with prisoners but these men were totally bewildered. They didn't seem to know what was going on so we sat them at the back of the trench, gave them some cigarettes and told them that if they moved we'd shoot them. They didn't move.

Soldier 3rd Battalion 505th Regiment

These men were soldiers in the true sense of the word. The 82nd were veterans of Sicily and Salerno. They had a job to do and they set about doing it. If they hadn't the numbers they had expected, they made do with what they did have. They gathered into groups under the leadership of an officer or sergeant and moved out. Their disorganization had an advantage that none of them had envisaged. The Germans didn't have an idea about what was going on.

Captain Gibbons landed safely but he was on his own. He was completely disoriented and spent his first hour trying to get his bearings. Then he saw a movement and clicked his cricket.

I got a two click answer and suddenly I felt a thousand years younger. To my surprise, he was not from my plane. He wasn't even from my division. We moved on to our collection point and I blew my whistle. We had fifty men in no time but only fifteen were from the 506th.

I heard this cricket the other side of the hedge but I wasn't going to give myself away. I wanted to make sure it wasn't a Jerry there so I said the password, "Flash" and straight away the answer came, "Thunder." He was one of us.

At 01.40. hours 27 of the 36 sticks of parachutists of the 2nd battalion landed on or near their targeted point. Lt. Col. Benjamin Vandervoort broke his ankle as he landed but he tied his boot tighter round his ankle and used his rifle as a walking stick and rallied the men. He sent up green flares to tell his men where he was and, within half an hour, 600 men had reached him. Their mission was to secure Neuville au Plain, north of St Mere Eglise. It was a long way and Vandervoort saw two sergeants pulling a collapsible ammunition cart and he asked them for a lift but they told him they hadn't brought it all that way to carry some Goddam officer. He persuaded them otherwise.

In spite of the bad drop, men began to collect in small groups. They knew what the targets were and they went for them. If they couldn't get to their own rendezvous, then they joined another group. If that wasn't possible, they would collect in small groups of their own, attacking and setting up road blocks. These men were ready to fight and they fought. There was no chance for them to destroy the Douve Bridges but they were undaunted. They attacked and harried and they achieved everything that had been expected of them. One group killed Major General Falley, the Commander of the German 91st Division. General Ridgway commented that he couldn't see why the death of a General should give the men such pleasure but his death was a stroke of luck for the allies. One group put the German Battle Headquarters out of action. They attacked time and time again so that the whole of the 91st Division was on the defensive for days. They had no time to spare for the troops landing on the beaches.

There were more aircraft going over than usual and I thought there was a heavy raid going on but what I couldn't understand was the bursts of gun fire behind us. I doubled the guard and sent a patrol out to reconnoitre. They were back in no time with this parachutist who had landed on the beach alongside them. It seemed the rest of his stick had landed in the sea and were shouting for help but it was quiet when I went out. My men brought in nineteen prisoners altogether. I locked them in a pill box and put a guard in front. I phoned my battalion commander and, as I started to talk, the line went dead. I knew the invasion would only come on a high tide and in two hours time it would be low tide. Four o'clock in the morning, my guard reported to me that the prisoners were insisting on being moved further back from the beaches. I couldn't understand why.

German officer.

Our glider made a perfect landing at 07.10 hours and we made for the landing zone. The team had already captured eight German soldiers. I went across to interrogate them but they didn't seem to understand German so I tried Russian. The response was immediate.
"Ya, Ya, we want to go to America."
"Me too," I said.

L Mendel 325 Glider Infantry

We were walking along this hedge when I heard rustling at my feet. A woman and two little children crawled out of the ditch. She pointed at a house in front of us and said, "Bosch, Bosch." We soon had it surrounded after I'd given her some chocolate bars for the children. A lot of the French people were hiding out in the country that night. We had to be careful.

Tony de Fay - F Company

The Americans had been unable to take the bridges over the Merderet, because only 22 of the expected 52 expected gliders had materialized so they didn't have the equipment they needed but they strengthened the road blocks and cut the communications.

The 101st was more fortunate. The 506th regiment had landed on target and two battalions attacked the most southern exits from Utah beach. They immediately started to clear the area. By dawn, they had taken all five causeways and three battery positions further north. They were lucky because fifty of their gliders carrying guns, ammunition and signalling equipment landed at the right place. But they were unable to take the Douve bridges north of Carentan because they were being defended by the German's toughest troops, their 6th Parachute Regiment. The Americans did not have enough men to challenge them but they didn't give them that impression. They attacked and were driven back time and time again, until the invasion force was controlling the Normandy beaches.

Although the American Commanders thought their landings had been a fiasco, they had achieved everything that Montgomery had wanted. The landings on Utah were protected; the German 91st Division and the 6th Parachute Regiment were fighting for the bridges rather than counter attacking and numerous small parties were roaming the countryside like a lot of gangsters, attacking the enemy wherever they appeared. They pinned down ten times their own numbers in futile and frustrating activities. The Germans became more and more confused.

The Germans had rounded up eleven of us and this German officer started to question us. He spoke perfect English and it was obvious he hadn't any idea what we were doing there. He kept asking how many of us had landed. We told him, millions and millions. He wanted to know why we had different badges on our uniforms and we told him we liked the pictures. He wasn't pleased with our answers. Then they brought in another one of us. He was an Italian American and he was chewing gum. The Germans had difficulty spelling his name and he didn't help, kept adding a letter or telling them one was in the wrong place. Then came the question. How many of us were there. "Just me," he said innocently. I think if he had a gun ready, the officer would have shot us all.

Field Marshal Erwin Rommel did not consider the conditions right for an allied invasion. The men had been stood down on the fifth of June and many of the officers had taken the opportunity to go home. The bad weather had lulled them into a false sense of security. Even Admiral Krancke, the Naval Commander at Cherbourg had cancelled the night's reconnaissance patrol by the E boat flotilla. At 01.11 hours

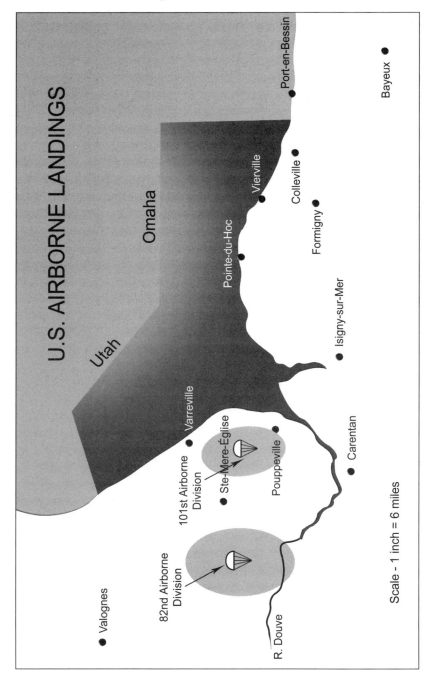

U.S. AIRBORNE LANDINGS

Scale - 1 inch = 6 miles

General Marcks received a message from General Richter that paratroops were landing East of the River Orne. Then came more reports of similar landings from all over Normandy. Many of these proved to be straw and rubber dolls with crackers built into them that were activated when they landed and sounded like machine gun fire.

The R.A.F. had been very active up to the day of the invasion and there was always this aim to deceive. The final part of the deception plan involved Bomber Command. They had been bombing two targets outside the landing zone to every one inside it. No. 100 group carried out ABC (Airborne Cigar jamming), jamming ground stations as well as attacking the German radar sites and communication networks. The combination of jamming provided a complete screen and was known as the Mandrell system. It needed to be in place from the evening of the 4th and was provided by Flying Fortresses of the 803rd Squadron of the American Eighth Bomber Command and 19 Stirlings from 199 Squadron.

The first drop of the dummy parachutists was between Coutances and St. Lo in the early hours of June 6th. They were dropped through a screen of window, (strips of silver paper) These were followed by many others dropped over a wide area. The idea was to draw the enemy's radar attention away from and confuse the Germans about the whereabouts of the real parachute drops.

Despite Marck's urgent signals,. the German Army Command refused to be hurried into making a decision. The German officers disagreed amongst themselves as to whether this was the expected invasion but most thought that Rommel was right and it was a diversion. Some of the officers lacked imagination and were reluctant to move without orders. Orders had been given that Panzer Divisions were not to advance without Hitler's permission. Runstedt spent vital hours trying to contact Hitler and get permission to move troops. No permission was forthcoming. Hitler was in bed and none of his staff would rouse him.

Rommel's absence from Normandy at the time of the invasion was the best news the allies could have received. None welcomed it more than Admiral Ramsay who had remarked that they had a fairly large job to do. Not only did they have to move something the size of Birmingham from one country to another, they had to keep it moving.

The Naval and Air bombardments started at 05.30 hours and the first landing craft reached the beaches at 06.31 hours.

GOLD BEACH

The 1st Hampshires, the 1st Dorsets, the 6th Green Howards and the 5th East Yorks were the four Assault Battalions that made up the first wave of the invasion on Gold Beach. Montgomery had said that he wanted battle experienced soldiers to go in on this first wave.

The Green Howards and East Yorks target was to make for Crepon. They went to take the bridge over the river and reach the road between Bayuex and Caen to prevent enemy movements along it. (They did so on the morning of the 7th June).

The Devon's and Hampshire's target was Bayeux. They almost made it on D Day but the job was completed the following morning.

Although the Germans had been expecting the invasion they had no real idea when or where it was likely to happen. The German Army had changed its purpose from attacking to managing the countries it had captured and to protecting and guarding the coastlines of those countries. This was particularly true of France where they expected the invasion to take place. The Atlantic Wall had been built to guard the shores. The German troops were stretched to man these defences. Normandy was a comfortable posting for most of the German soldiers. Many of those who had been wounded or fought on the Eastern Front were stationed along the Atlantic Wall as were captured Poles, Russians and others from Eastern Europe that were used as forced labour. Elderly men and members of the Hitler Youth also had the honour of fighting for the Fuhrer. Many of these were stationed along the Normandy coast. But there were still strong German fighting Divisions in the area. The crack 352nd Division was commanded by General Dietrich Kraiss. He was sure that his troops would be able to repel the allies but he lacked reserves. The eastern flank had opened up the road to Bayeux and Kraiss called up the LXXXIV Corps reserves, the 915th reserve that had been billeted in Bayeux but they had been sent out in the early morning to deal with the reported parachute landings, some of which turned out to be the straw dolls that the R.A.F, had been dropping as decoys. Kraiss wasted over an hour contacting the unit. The French saboteurs had been at work and most of the communication lines had been cut. When they did receive the orders, they moved immediately. A collection of old French lorries, bicycles and men on foot started off but it was more than three hours before the first of them was near enough to counter attack.

I was a pilot of a Hurricane fighter. We'd been flying sorties since daybreak. Our orders were to attack any planes from the Luftwaffe that approached the Normandy beaches and take any steps that were necessary to stop German reserves moving up to the battle zones. I didn't see any German planes and it was some time before I saw these German troops moving towards the coast in these old lorries and cars. Some of the men were riding in line on bicycles and behind them were marching troops. We dived in and gave them a bit of their own medicine that they had meted out at Dunkirk. Went in with our guns firing. Within seconds there wasn't a man in sight, they'd made for the ditches at the side of the road. We waited until they started to return and then we went in again and again. We kept them pinned down and as we peeled off to return to base, three Spitfires were flying in to take over. We had to report anything suspicious that we saw on the ground. I reported what could have been a petrol dump near a railway yard but somebody had already alerted Bomber Command. I saw these three Typhoons flying in like bats out of hell and as we reached the coast on our way home, I saw another plume of black smoke rising into the air.

F.O. J. Smythe. R.A.F.

They brought the 50th Division back in 1943 from the Mediterranean. They were hardened soldiers. They had been fighting continuously for four years and I wanted to be one of them. It was said that these men were to be the spearhead of the second front. My requests were turned down. I went and saw our Sergeant Major, Squeaker Bennett. He had a face like a pickled walnut. He listened to my request and handed me an envelope. I could put my corporal's stripe in there if I really wanted to go because I would be demoted to a private. He didn't think I would do it but I did. I was posted to the 5th Battalion Holding Company at Aldershot. We were to be reinforcements for the 5th East Yorks. We were loaded in lorries and taken to Canning Town in the east end of London and pitched our tents in empty bombed streets. I had never seen such devastation, yet people were living in these broken shells of houses. Then a heavy fence was put round the camp and we were shut in. Red Caps appeared to guard the camp and we were paraded and told we must not talk to anyone outside the camp. We were also told that the Second front was about to start. We weren't told where it would be but we knew it was France. We were paid in French francs that had been especially minted for the invasion.

Three days later, we were paraded with full kit and marched down to East India Docks where we boarded an old peace time troop ship. We set sail almost immediately. As we passed Southend Pier, one of the men jumped overboard and swam for it. We all cheered him and carried on cheering long after he was lost to view. We were anchored out at sea for a week and we were bored stiff. One morning an elderly officer came on board. He had been in the First World War and wore a Military Cross amongst others. Eight of us were to be transferred to another ship. The old officer watched us leave with tears in his eyes. I realized long afterwards that he thought he was sending us to our deaths.

We reached an L.C.I. (Landing Craft Infantry) with assault craft slung over the sides where one usually saw lifeboats. We clambered up a rope ladder and were welcomed by C.O. Colonel White. He told me I would be in Sergeant Mayhew's platoon and he arrived almost immediately. He took me below and handed me over to Corporal Stevenson who told me I would be a rifleman in his section. "Stick by me," he said, "and you'll be alright."

I was in a different world. All the men were wearing campaign ribbons and they were so calm. They were real men, real soldiers and I felt elated to be amongst them. They were happy and cheerful and confident. They spent a lot of time betting with their invasion money, playing cards or talking. One of their favourite subjects was women and they would look at me and grin at the expression on my face and say, "Don't worry. You'll soon learn."

The officers, warrant officers and N.C.O.s spent a lot of time in meetings. Then we were all mustered on deck. That was when we

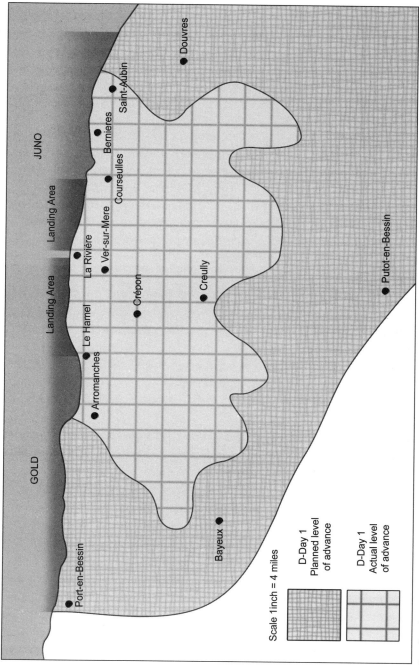

Douvres

Saint-Aubin

Bernières

Courseulles

JUNO

Landing Area

Ver-sur-Mere

La Rivière

Landing Area

Le Hamel

Arromanches

GOLD

Port-en-Bessin

Crépon

Creully

Putot-en-Bessin

Bayeux

Scale 1inch = 4 miles

D-Day 1
Planned level
of advance

D-Day 1
Actual level
of advance

Landing Areas - Gold & Juno Beaches

were told that this was the invasion and what was expected of us. The C.O. said that not much opposition was expected. That caused a lot of laughter from the veterans. We were to advance inland and we weren't to stop for anyone or anything, not even wounded men. There were others coming behind us who were trained to deal with them.

"Whatever happens, don't stop advancing," we were told. "We go in at first light tomorrow."

The atmosphere on the ship changed. There was still the same camaraderie amongst the men but it was quieter and the men were more careful with their speech. I didn't hear a single swear word. None of them teased the padre now. There was none of, "Here comes the padre, count your money lads." He moved amongst the men talking quietly. Some of the battle hardened men asked to see him privately. Cards and crown and anchor boards were pushed to one side The men were almost gentle with each other. They were preparing for the following day.

"Have you had a shower?" one of them asked me. "Make sure you do."

I wasn't keen on showers. They were salt water and the soap didn't lather but I did what I was told.

"Make sure you wear clean underclothes and socks. You'll be less likely to get infection in if you're wounded."

"Don't ever think of taking risks. A dead hero is no use to anyone."

We assembled on deck at 03.30. hours. Ammunition for rifles and light machine guns was distributed. Grenades were issued and primed with four second fuses, two grenades to each man, Each man had a no. 75 Hawkins anti tank grenade to fasten to his belt. We had packs on our backs as well as bags containing our gas masks. Corporal Stevenson checked that I was alright. He took my gas mask out and threw it overboard and filled the bag with more ammunition. "That'll be more use to you than a gas mask," he said.

It was pitch dark. There were no lights on board yet the soldiers moved round with confidence. Dawn was beginning to break as we climbed into the landing craft ready to be lowered to the sea. The waves were running high and I wasn't the only one who was beginning to wish that I hadn't eaten such a hearty breakfast. Until that moment, everything had happened in complete silence As we left the mother ship bound for Gold Beach, Red King section, the naval guns started up You can't see out of a landing craft, the sides are too high, but you can hear and there's no word in the vocabulary that can describe the noise that morning, the whistle and explosions of the shells, the roar of the rockets as they left the rocket ships, the sound of the waves and men shouting through megaphones, planes screaming overhead, appearing and disappearing within seconds.

We didn't talk, nobody would have heard us against that noise. I wasn't frightened, just very excited. Men around me were being sick and the scuppers were full of vomit I don't think I had ever felt so ill in my life. Then there was a grinding sound and the craft hit the beach. The ramp dropped down almost immediately and the men left in two lines. The craft was slipping back into the sea very slowly. I was behind the sergeant when the marine put his arm in front of me. "Hold on a minute, son," he said and the engines started and ran up on to the sand. I don't know what happened to the sergeant. He disappeared. I reckoned the ramp must have run over him. He couldn't have got out of the way with all his kit. Then I was moving forward on to the French beaches. There was a landing craft coming in beside us with an officer at the front with a megaphone reciting Henry the V's speech at Agincourt, " Once more into the breach dear friends...." Planes were screaming overhead and the naval guns were booming so that they echoed inside my head. I was running over the sand. It's strange how one's mind works because I was thinking of the days I had spent on the beach as a child.I was sure the sergeant had been killed and it worried me. The beach was full of action. Men seemed to be running in all directions. The beach master was shouting through his megaphone. Then I saw the corporal signalling for us to make for the sea wall. I couldn't hear him in all that din but I understood the signals.

I reached the sea wall and leaned against it to regain my breath. Other soldiers were doing the same. That was when I realized that some of our men were absent. Looking back, I saw men lying on the sand. That gave me a shock. I hadn't realized we were being shot at. We wouldn't have heard the shots not with all that noise. I started to look round and I could hardly believe the sight in front of me. It was a hive of activity in every direction. Men were filing off landing craft and advancing up the beaches. L.C.T.s (Landing Craft Tanks) were on the tide line with their ramps open like huge gaping mouths. Tanks were beginning to trundle up the beaches. They had skirts on them to stop the water getting into their exhaust pipes which they dropped as they came on to the sand. Flail tanks were already at work clearing the beaches of mines. One poor devil trod on a mine as he ran up the beach and was blown to smithereens. Soldiers coming up behind him simply stepped over what had been a living being a few moments before. We had been lucky. The tide had carried us over the obstacles that the Germans had built in the water. The Canadians further along the beach had not been so lucky. Rommel's spaghetti, the angle iron traps, were exposed and men had been caught on them. The waves were washing over them and lifting them up so that they seemed to be dancing in the water but the faces that looked at us were dead. Aeroplanes were overhead, wave after wave of them and out at sea were the ships. It was difficult to see the horizon because they were so close together that they seemed to be fastened and the smoke blurred their outlines. There was constant movement with the small boats and landing craft. Our L.T.C. was backing off and turning round and, at that moment there was a terrific explosion. A tank had hit a mine and blew up. The men inside wouldn't have had a chance, the tank was a blazing inferno within seconds.

A sergeant was gasping at us, "Over the wall, over the wall."

We couldn't hear what he was saying but it was obvious that he wanted us to move. A soldier carrying a sten gun scrambled up the wall and I followed. We ran across the road and down the other side into scrub land on the other side. Paths were worn between the undergrowth and we started along one of them in single file. It seemed strangely peaceful after the frenetic activity on the beaches. That was when I saw my first Germans. There were ponds and marshy areas amongst the scrub and there were banks that crossed them. These two Germans started walking along the banks carrying a gun in two parts. They stopped when they saw us and then they started to run. Everyone fired at them. Our platoon fired from the hip. The Germans were quite dead when we walked past them.

I hated the Germans. It's hard for people to understand those feelings today. I didn't know anything about concentration camps or forced labour but I did know what the Nazis stood for and what they had done to other countries like Poland and Russia and Holland. I didn't hate the Germans as individuals, I hated what they stood for.

We were still making our way through the scrub but the Germans had woken up. We came under fire from small arms as well as mortar fire. Some men were wounded but it was the mines that caused the damage. Men were killed when they trod on one, others when a bomb landed in a minefield and caused sympathetic explosions. Men following on behind stopped just long enough to put the fallen man's rifle in the ground beside him. If he was dead, they would put his helmet on top of the gun. He had no further use for it. If he was wounded, only the rifle would stand up beside him. That made it easier for the stretcher bearers to get to those that they could help more quickly.

Our advance had slowed to a crawl but we were still going forward. We knew what our target was and we were making for it. The main thing that was hindering us was the number of Germans that were surrendering, mostly older men who had had enough but there were others who were going to fight to the death. The young soldiers were the worst. Even when they were captured, they proved difficult to handle. If the Germans came towards us carrying weapons, we shot them. We didn't trust any of them. We sent the others back to the beaches. There were men there who could deal with them.

Our main objective was the anti-tank gun at the village of La Riviere that had been detected by aerial photographs. It had to be destroyed. We had been told that the Navy would put it out of action but, if they failed, it was to be destroyed by a Petard. This is a high explosive carried on a tank and operated by Royal Engineers. Our job as infantryman was to make sure that the tank could get into position. Unfortunately both the navy and the Petard had failed and the anti tank gun was causing real damage. We had lost a lot of men and there was only one officer there, Captain Consett. He was everywhere, giving orders and instructions. The German gun knocked out the other tanks that had been brought up, three of them, one after the other, amphibious tanks from the 4th/ 7th Dragoon Guards. Then another tank came up and was directed by Captain Consett. He lead us in. The gun was silenced that time, taken by storm.

Rumours were always going round in the army and they didn't stop even in the middle of a battle. The Green Howards had landed alongside us. Stories about Stan Hollis were already circulating. He was the Sergeant Major. He and his officer realized they had passed a pill box and went back to make sure it was empty. When they were twenty yards away, a machine gun had started up and Stan had charged the pill box, recharging his magazine as he ran. He had killed two Germans and taken the rest prisoners. His action saved the Company and allowed them to open up the exits from the beach.

Later that day, they encountered a spandau (field gun) crew. Hollis lead an attack on it but they were held up. Hollis took cover in a house at which the spandau fired. Hollis ordered immediate evacuation and lead an attack on the gun emplacement. Two of his men were killed but the German gun was silenced. Then he learned that two of his crew were still in the house. In full view of the enemy, he went and rescued them. When you put that action into the noise and tension of the day, you can see that his V.C. was well deserved.

There was another rumour going round that our C.O., Lieutenant Colonel White had been seriously wounded and that B Company on our right had gained their objective, the village of Ver sur Mer and were advancing towards Crepon. Both these rumours proved to be true.

We were D company. We reformed and started moving forward but not before the Green Howards passed through our depleted lines. Two of the men had been in the Young Soldiers Battalion with me, Joe Turner and Taglioni. We said Hello as if we were passing each other in the street. We wished each other luck and moved on. I've never seen either of them again.

Some tanks had come up and we went forward in open order of extended line. We met scattered opposition but we moved on steadily. We took the village of St. Gabriel but we were beginning to slow down. We were tired almost to the point of exhaustion and the enemy resistance was getting stronger. We had reached the village of Brecy by nightfall, some way short of our objective. Corporal Stevenson told us to dig in near some farm buildings. There were only the Gates brothers, Jim and Billy that had made it that far besides the corporal and myself. Some said they weren't brothers, they just happened to have the same name but you never saw the two of them apart. They were both Geordies and they were never serious about anything. They were always cracking jokes. There were ten men in our section and four of us had survived. I discovered later that ten officers and 85 other ranks from our Regiment alone had perished on the beaches. Fifteen men from the three sections (that is 30 men) reported at the end of the day.

The corporal told me to dig in, in front of the farm gates and shoot at anything that moved. I wouldn't have slept anyway. I was tired but I was full of adrenaline. I hadn't eaten all day. I hadn't even taken my water bottle out. I'd drunk from streams or water butts, not a very sensible thing to do but when you're fighting, you don't think of sensible things. I took out my water bottle then and took a long, cool drink of real English water. It was the best drink I have ever had in my life.

As dawn broke the next morning, the two Gates brothers came and joined me and asked where the Corporal was and I told them he was checking things out at the farm. They burst out laughing.

"Check it out," said Billy. "There's two young lasses in there. He's doing some checking out."

I had a lot to learn.

Dick Bowen - East Yorks

Dick Bowen

It wasn't our job to take the beaches but to make a safe path across them so that the commandos and others following on behind us could make a quick advance to their targets. God knows how I made it to the sea wall but I did. I stopped to catch my breath and looked back. It was an incredible sight, the ships, the landing craft, men trying to make it across the beach, the noise, the smell of smoke and cordite and the mist lifting slowly giving the whole scene a dream like setting. I suppose we had landed along a half mile stretch of the beach and the area on either side of the landing was tranquil and peaceful.

Soldier - 5th Battalion East Yorks

I was the principal beachmaster on Gold Beach. We landed in the early hours of June 6th. Our job was to keep the beach clear of obstructions, to organise exits from the beach and, once the beaches had been taken, make sure all movements were carried out in an orderly manner. I stayed as beachmaster for 6 weeks - B. Whinney, Lt Commander

H.M.S. Warspite and H.M.S. Ramillies off the coast of Normandy. The bombardment was aimed at the German coastal batteries

Men of the 50th. Division storming Gold Beach 6th. June 1944.

Bobbin Tank

We knew we were approaching the coast when we passed two American bodies floating in the water. I was on an LCT (Landing Craft Tank) with a barrage balloon attached to the deck by wire. This was to stop enemy dive bombers. We landed at Vers sur Mer. I'd never seen anything like it. It was a mass of movement men and machines. The first vehicle off was a Sherman Tank. It went down the ramp slowly, then splash and it completely disappeared. The sand bank had hidden the deep pool behind. We fell about laughing. The men got out alright and we shouted encouragement. They were not amused.

I walked off on to the beach. The beachmaster was a big bearded Naval Officer. I asked him what I should do. He told me in real naval terms. I found my CO purely by chance.

"Good," he said, "Now we've got an explosives expert."

I looked at him, "I'm a fitter armourer," I said, "I don't know anything about explosives."

"Then you'd better learn."

I learned.

We had to check everything that had been damaged. All defective bombs and ammunition had to be destroyed. I had to find somewhere safe where they could be blown up. I soon had a good system going. We would line a pit with rocket boxes and block one end, fill the space with suspect explosives, put a rocket tube down one end put the ammunition on top, add a few rounds of 303s. Pour a couple of gallons of petrol over the lot. Throw a light down the tunnel and run.

Ian Smith - Royal Engineers

We had the RAF with us all the time we were in action. They didn't land with us on the beaches but by the time we were digging in alongside us. There were two of them, an officer who carried a thing that looked like a broken umbrella. When they were in action, he would put it up and it would act as an aerial. His airman would carry the radio. When we were in difficulty he would call up the aircraft and in would come the rocket firing Typhoons. They never missed their target. A tank would be crippled in seconds.

We approached a wooded area and it looked as though Christmas had come. The trees were decorated with glistening silver strips. The window that the RAF had dropped to confuse the German RADAR had caught in *the trees and undergrowth and the whole area sparkled in the evening sunlight.*

The Germans had an 88mm artillery gun that put the fear of God into us. It was accurate and deadly. It was a three purpose gun that fired a $3^1/_2$ inch Shell, anti-aircraft, anti-tank and a basic field gun. We feared that gun as much as we feared the Tiger Tanks.

. . . .

I was called up in early 1939 and when they found out I could drive. I was sent to Bovington for training and that was how I found myself driving a tank and being part of the 11th Armoured Division. There were five of us in a tank crew, the commander who would be looking out of the turret and instructing us, the driver (me) and the gunner to my left and behind us, the radio operator and the soldier manning the heavy gun.

Come the beginning of 1944, we moved up near Gt. Yarmouth, Fritton Lakes and that was when we saw our first DD (Duplex Drive) Sherman tank. We'd never seen anything like it or heard of floating tanks but if we had to drive them through water, that's what we did. A week later, Sergeant Baker turned up from Bovington and told us he was going to show us how to drive them. We soon told him that it would be us showing him. We had been driving them through the lakes for the past week. They were no problem to drive, the problem was steering them. We would pinpoint a landmark like a Church spire and aim at that. We would have a gyro compass between our legs like they have on a boat.

A DD Tank was fitted with a canvas screen fixed to a boat shaped framework welded round the tank. We had a compressor which pumped compressed air through rubber pipes which lifted the canvas skirt vertically and provided a waterproof screen round the tank which allowed it to float giving it a one metre freeboard. If the canvas split you could be in trouble.

The tank was driven by twin propellors at the back of the tank. On reaching land, the screen was collapsed but on D Day several tank commanders collapsed the front of the screen while they were still in the water so that the big guns could be used.

Once we were competent in Fritton Lakes, we went for further training in the Thames Estuary. We also learned how to use the breathing bottles with which we were issued. These gave us five minutes to escape should the tank sink.

At the end of May, we moved down to the south coast. We'd never seen anything like it, lines and lines of tanks, lorries, jeeps, hundreds and hundreds of them

I was in the Royal Hussars and it was the 13/18 that went in in the DD tanks on Sword beach. We went in later on Gold Beach. By the time we landed the way across the beach had been cleared.

The Commander told me to turn to the left. I don't know what sixth sense told me to veer to the right. It was a good job I did because the gunner knocked out 7 anti-tank guns. If we'd veered to the left we'd have veered into their line of fire.

Later on, the Commander told us to stand down for ten minutes. We stood chatting beside the tank when there was an almighty bang. We dropped to the ground. As we stood up, I realised my friend Brian Cornwall had been killed and my tunic was splattered with his blood. His hair was standing straight up. It must have been the shock - I'd never seen anything like it. He was literally inches away from me. We were all stunned. Two young French girls ran across to help and Brian's body was taken away for burial. We still visit the grave and meet the two ladies who have continued to look after his grave.

L/Cpl Peter Smith

L/Cpl Peter Smith

Cromwell Tank which Peter drove later in the campaign

L/Cpl Peter Smith and comrades in Normandy

Veterans visiting Brian Cornwell's grave

Serjeant Hepper was commander of a DD (Swimming) tank landing on Gold Beach. The current was strong and he hit the beach higher up than he should have done. He closed in on a barrier of anti-tank, obstacles fitted with mines. There wasn't time to hesitate. There was a platoon following so he made for a gap and then another.

Their troubles weren't over. The Germans were dug in, so they brought the tank up and attacked.

Serjeant R Hepper 13/18 Royal Hussars
Serjeant Hepper was awarded the Military Medal for this action.

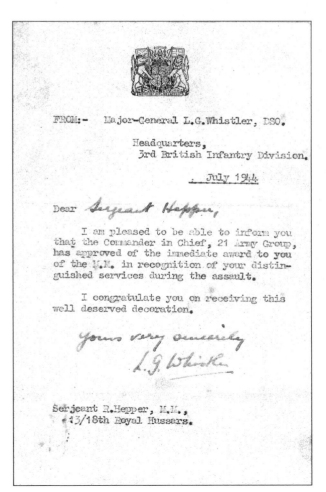

Letter to Serjeant Hepper from the Commander in Chief, 21 Army Group

Montgomery presenting the Military Medal to Serjeant Hepper 30th November 1944. (inset)
Serjeant Hepper

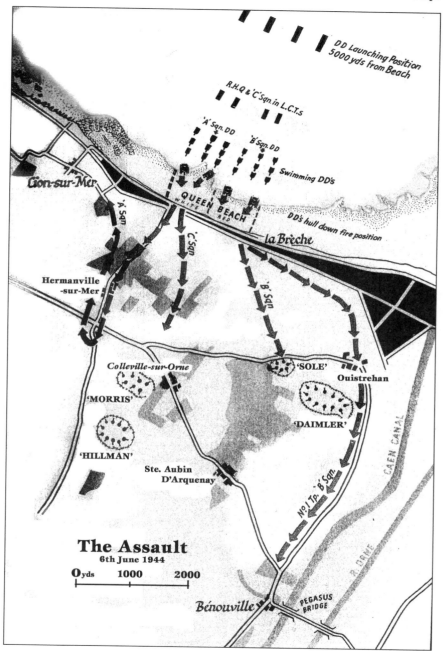

DD Tank Assault plan showing the projected advance for DD tanks

DD tank shedding its skirt as it approaches land

The skirt that protected this tank has become flooded and it is sinking. The crew are waiting to be rescued

I was a platoon Commander of The Durham Light Infantry. It was a rough trip into the landing beach and we could hear the noise of fighting ahead of us. Most of the men were sick and it was a relief when the L.C.T. slowed down and the ramp went down. I led the men off. The craft was still edging forward and the sea seemed shallow enough when I took my first step, but down I went. I was completely submerged and my boots filled with water. I realized the craft was still moving forward and I was likely to get run over if I didn't get a move on. I shed everything I could, kicked my boots off and threw my folding bicycle away and made for dry land. I tried to get to my feet but the waves were terrific and I was bowled over. I invaded France on my hands and knees.

The Commandos were specialist troops. They came into Normandy after the beaches had been captured. They had the specialist jobs to do. They had specific targets to meet.

We landed at 09.30 hours on Gold Beach, our target to make for and capture Port en Bessin and meet up with the Americans who had landed on Omaha. There was still fighting on the beaches along to our left but we had a pretty clear run across to the sea wall where we collected. The beach master shouted for us to move on but Colonel Phillips had everything under control. We set off along the coast road and we were being shot at from the start but we didn't slow down. We'd got our orders. We had to make for Port au Bessin and capture it before nightfall. We lost a lot of men to the Germans. They reckoned there was a dead marine every seventy yards along that road. I would have liked to pay them back but we had our orders. We had to move but we bided our time.. We had to take shelter from time to time and take a long route round in several places where the Germans were in a strong position. We reached Port au Bessin as night fell. We went in at first light the next morning.

N.C.O. 47 Royal Marines Commando

The coast road, Delta 514 is the memorial to the many members of 47 Marine Commandos that were killed along its length on the 6th June, 1944.

Port en Bessin was important. That was where PLUTO (Pipe line under the Ocean) was coming ashore. Supply of fuel to the allied forces was a problem the services had faced from the beginning. Petrol could be carried in jerry cans but they were difficult to transport. A pipeline under the ocean seemed to be the answer. The first one they tested had proved a dismal failure but the engineers worked on it and Pluto became one of the success stories of the invasion. The pipe carried fuel across the Solent to the isle of Wight. It went overland across the island and then beneath the Channel to Port en Bessin.

The French Resistance had been active in the weeks leading up to D day. The R.A.F. had dropped thousands of weapons to them in the days leading up to Operation Overlord. On the 5th of June, the B.B.C. had sent out coded messages telling them that the invasion would be next day. That afternoon and evening members of the Resistance visited the homes of those that could be trusted, warning them to take cover and stay indoors the next day.

I had been forewarned that the invasion would be soon and I had sent my wife and children to stay with their aunt inland. The noise in the early morning was incredible and I walked across to the cliffs to see what was happening. I couldn't get close to the edge because of the mines but I stood on a wall and the sight that met my eyes was one that will stay in my memory for the rest of my days. There were ships of every shape and size lined up and overhead the sky was dark with aeroplanes and I knew that this was the beginning of the end of the occupation for the French people.

Shopkeeper at Arromanches

There had been bombing raids along the coast and bombardment from ships in the Channel for some weeks so we had dug a trench in the back garden. We sheltered in that when the bombing got really bad. Mother was living with us and wouldn't let us go there until we had eaten. Then a shell came through the wall and we ran to the trench.

It was a good job we did because the windows and walls of the house were badly damaged. My friend had wanted us to go with her inland but I could not leave our house. My husband and eldest son were fighting with the Maquis in southern France. They wouldn't have known where to find us. There was a pause in the bombing attacks about four o'clock in the morning and two of the children took the opportunity to run indoors for something. When they came out, my son climbed on to the wall to see what was happening. Then he started shouting, "Mummy. Mummy. The sea's black with boats." I knew that the invasion had started.

Mme du Pont

. . . .

Returning from a sortie over France we couldn't doubt that the invasion was imminent. We couldn't miss the huge Armada that was gathering along the south coast and the thousands of ships which were still converging from east and west.

The briefings around midnight were unforgetable. Electric with anticipation, we cheered when it was announced that British and American paratroopers were already dropping around vital targets in Normandy. There was little sleep that night. The first squadrons were off in the night.

We crossed the Channel which was full of ships of every description. We headed inland searching the roads for reinforcements on the move but there were none. We saw some light flak from a wooded area so we rocketed and strafed it but there was nothing to see - great disappointment.

Other sorties were timed to soften up the beach defences as the first landing craft were going in. The naval bombardment was in full swing. Rocket armed fighters were firng in salvo after salvo. The Typhoons joined in with delay action bombs and hosing the defences with cannon.

Apart from a few specific targets, the Typhoons provided close support for the landings and armed reconnaisance but the attackers were moving inland at widely varying distances. There was no bombline, no front line and we were in danger of attacking our own troops, so we switched to reconnaisance.

By the end of D-day, 400 Typhoon sorties had been flown at the cost of eight aircraft, 4 to enemy fighters and 4 to flak and debris.

Our target was to take out the enemy HQ which we did in style. The French Resistance let us know when the funerals of the officers who had been killed were taking place. We gave them time to get started and went in and got a few more of them.

....

We went in to attack some German tanks and the Germans got out and ran when they saw us diving towards them.

Typhoon pilots

Fighters and small bombers carried the invasion markings, black and white stripes around the wings and fuselage.

....

We'd been married for 11 glorious weeks. Max flew a Mosquito. He was a New Zealander and I was a WAAF which is how we met. I knew he'd been killed when his plane hadn't returned but it wasn't until I was called into the CO's office that I knew for sure. It was a long time after that I found out that his plane had been shot down but he parachuted out and the Germans had shot him as he came down. Our daughter was born nine months later. He never knew he was going to be a father.

His parents came over after the war. Max was their only child. They wanted to take Gillian back over with them but they didn't want me. I didn't marry again, not until Gillian was married with a family of her own.

I never went to see Max's grave. I couldn't face it. Then 50 years later we were returning to England by coach and there had been an accident on the main road and we were diverted and stopped at a village for coffee. Everyone got off but I couldn't move. "Where did you say we are?" I asked the driver and then I told him, "My husband's buried here."

I found his grave and I wept. I'd never been able to weep before. The coach driver must have told the others. They bought all the flowers in the flower shop and covered Max's grave and they collected flowers from other graves and added them as well.

That was when I said goodbye.

Joan Poole WAAF

If we could have surrendered to those rocket bearing typhoons, we would have done. They put the fear of God into us.

German POW

A Mosquito

A painting of a Typhoon
by Pete West

69

BBC Broadcast

*O*f enemy troop movements there was, until noon today, little or no sign from the air, even close to the battle area. Long stretches of empty roads shining with rain, deserted dripping woods and damp fields - static, quiet, - perhaps uncannily quiet - and possibly not to remain quiet. But here and there a movement catches the eye as our aircraft of reconnaissance roar over a large suspicious wood - three German soldiers running like mad across the main road to fling themselves into cover. And near the battle area, much nearer the battle area than they, a solitary peasant harrowing his field, up and down behind the horses looking nowhere but before him and the soil.

Richard Dimbleby of the B.B.C. reporting the invasion while accompanying an R.A.F. Reconnaissance flight.

*I*was seventeen years old. I had been in the Hitler Youth since I was ten years old and I was proud to be a soldier for the Fuhrer. I thought I would be a fighting soldier but I was posted to Normandy and spent most of the time on guard duty on the coast. I was due to be relieved at seven o'clock. It was a damp dismal day and a wind was blowing off the sea and whipping up the waves. The horizon was hidden by mist. As the sun rose in the sky, so the mist started to lift and as it cleared, I saw the ships, more and more ships until I couldn't see anything else and, at that moment, their guns started to fire and I thought my ear drums would burst and the sky grew dark with the planes flying over head. I was shouting and running to the blockhouse. I've never been so scared in my life.

H. Schmidt.

By midnight, the 50th Division had accomplished its main objectives. The beach head had been secured and troops and equipment could be brought ashore safely. The main road had been cut making movement difficult for the Germans and they had captured the little port of Arromanches. There had been no heavy bombing at Arromanches. The allies knew that lack of a reliable harbour would hold up the advance after the invasion. Arromanches had been selected to provide this safe harbour.

I was in the navy. On May 31st, I was ordered to report to Chatham where I was kitted out with army uniform. The only thing I was allowed to keep was my hat and I was issued with a khaki cover for that. We reported to Fareham and were taken to Stokes Bay jetty and embarked on H.M.S. Despatch. We were told on June 4th that the invasion had been delayed by bad weather and we would be going the following day. In fact, we went in on the 6th. We arrived off Arromanches at four o'clock but had to wait while they cleared out the last of the Germans. The worst of the fighting on the beaches was over but we were still mesmerized by what was going on around us. I don't think the Chef or I spoke a word. There was so much to see, boats of every size and description, boats as far as you could see. The first of the block ships were in place, ships that were being sunk and allowed to settle to provide breakwaters and provide a calm harbour area. This was code named Gooseberry.

We had to climb into a landing craft to go ashore. We were told the doors would open on to the sand and we could walk ashore. That didn't happen. The first men found themselves up to their necks in the water and some of the smaller ones had to swim for it. Chef and I looked at each other and thumbed a lift on a DUKW (an amphibian vehicle)

The beach master directed us to a house along the front and told us to prepare it for the captain. We didn't know who the captain was but we started to get the house ready. We had expected it to be Captain Petrie who had been with us on the Despatch but his duties had been changed. There was no furniture in the house and we had to scrounge everything we needed. A destroyer had been damaged and beached so we got a good deal from that. Then the Chef found a charcoal kitchen stove in a damaged house and we started lugging that back when the Chef looked up and said, "What the hell's that?" We looked out to sea and there were these tugs on the horizon towing this great contraption that must have been 80 feet high and it was towed right into Arromanches and we could see another great block coming in behind it. We weren't the only ones standing there. Lots of people had come down to the front and were standing there staring. That was the first time we heard the word Mulberry. Not all the sections were as tall as the first one we'd seen. Each section was towed in over the next few days and slotted into its proper place. Within days, the Mulberry Harbour was in use. Captain Petrie directed the building of the Mulberry Harbour. Captain Hickling was responsible for the running and organization of it. He was the captain for whom we had prepared the house and Chef and I had to manage it for him and for the many guests who came to visit and see this engineering feat in action.

Allan Walker. R.N.

The suggestion for an artificial harbour was proposed at the Quebec Conference and it was agreed that two harbours should be built and transported across the Channel in sections, one for the American Forces and one for the British sector. They were code named Mulberry. Without a harbour it would have been impossible to keep the forces supplied with sufficient necessities. These harbours would have to handle 2,500 vehicles a day, 12,000 tons of cargo and be able to cope with the 26 foot draught of the Liberty ships. They would have to provide safe anchorage for smaller ships in bad weather and have a minimum life of three months. By then, the allies planned to have captured a French port. Each harbour section was to be ready by May 1st 1944, seven months to build two harbours each the size of Dover. They were of such strong construction that remnants of the Mulberry Harbour at Arromonche can still be seen. Unfortunately the American harbour was damaged too badly in a storm to be used but it had not been as important as expected because supplies could be carried across the beaches of Utah. The Mulberry Harbour at Arromanche was one of the success stories of the invasion.

Allan Walker joined the Navy in 1939. He was in various actions. While in a Convoy to Malta, his ship, The Manchester was torpedoed. He became a prisoner of the Vichy French and was imprisoned in the notorious Laghouat Fort, released when the Allies invaded Algiers, Allan had 5 weeks leave and returned to duty in Britain and trained for his role on D-Day.

Mulberry Docks

JUNO and SWORD

The First Corps assault was on a larger scale and went in on two beaches, Juno and Sword.. These beaches were separated by five miles of rocky coastline which was heavily protected by the Germans. The third Canadian Division and the 2nd Canadian Armoured brigade went in on Juno. Their target was to get eleven miles in-land and to capture the airfield at Carpiquet. The beach on which they were to land was exposed and it was known that the shoreline was full of obstacles and that the beach had been heavily mined. The tide was running high and many of these obstacles were already submerged and there was little the frogmen could do before the first wave of Canadians were due to land twenty minutes later. They did their best, trying to remove and dismantle the obstacles often in twenty feet of water but they had only cleared a fraction when the first landing craft appeared. Some craft were blown up, others had to drop the men out at sea. The Irish Canadian Sergeant McQuaid was heard shouting, "Oh the evil of it, trying to drown me before I've even got to the beach."

I was with the Regina Rifle Regiment and I discovered I'd volunteered for just about the worst job there was, to go in early on the beaches and blow up the beach obstacles. Funny because I don't agree with volunteering for anything but there you are and there was I waiting on the L.S.T. with orders to keep the Major alive. I'd never seen anything like it, there we were heading for Mike sector, Juno Beach and they were using their time to sharpen their knives or play poker and that wasn't for small stakes either. Some of those knives were the sharpest I'd ever seen and still they sat there sharpening the blades on their whetstones. Then we saw this single ship steaming through the convoy and there was this piper playing a lament on the bagpipes, "Will ye no Come Back Again." That got to me that did.

We were off loaded on to an L.C.A. (Landing Craft Assault) and started the run in. As we approached the beach, some of the craft set off the Teller mines. They weren't big enough to do a lot of damage

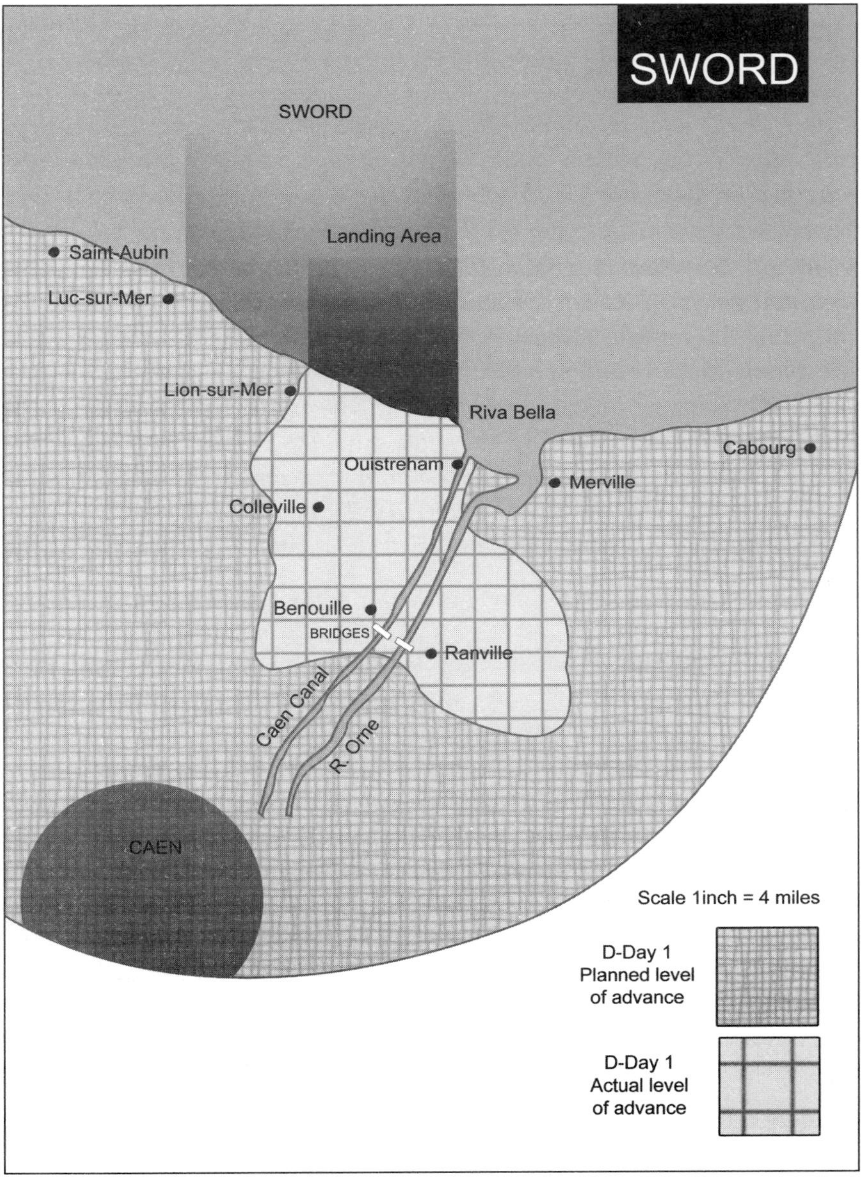
SWORD
SWORD
Landing Area
Saint-Aubin
Luc-sur-Mer
Lion-sur-Mer
Riva Bella
Ouistreham
Cabourg
Merville
Colleville
Benouille
BRIDGES
Ranville
Caen Canal
R. Orne
CAEN
Scale 1inch = 4 miles
D-Day 1
Planned level
of advance
D-Day 1
Actual level
of advance

but they were big enough to hole the boats or damage the ramps. We finished up by running into one of them and the Major says, "I'm going over," and he did. There was nothing for me but to go over after him. I didn't dare let him out of my sight. He said he'd cut the wires and I said I'd go for the detonators. I had to wrap my legs round the tetrahedron and started to unscrew the detonators. The Major was shouting for the men to get off the craft and go to the stern and lift the prow off the obstacle. I gave them a hand and we got our shoulders to it and got it off. It was about 08.00 hours and the first L.C.A.s were dropping the assault teams and they were making their way up on to the beach. Snipers and mortar crews were aiming towards the landing craft. We were sitting ducks out there. My mates were attacking the pill boxes. That was their job. After a while I went and joined my friends sheltering by the sea wall. A couple of the chaps helped me up and over. The guns quietened after a while and French people started appearing and throwing flowers at us. Then the barber came along and offered me some cognac.

Canadian Soldier

....

Enlisted in the West Yorkshire Regiment. Served in 'B' Company, 2nd Battalion, the East Yorkshire Regiment, on D day. Wounded on D day and evacuated to UK.

Photo shows Ron Major, back in the UK enjoying a cup of tea provided by the Womens' Voluntary Services who cared for the wounded from D day as they arrived back from the beachhead.

Pte Ronald Major

We went in on Juno in the second wave. We landed at a little sea side place called Bernieres. I reckon this spot I'm standing on now is the very place I came ashore all those years ago. I said I'd never come back, I lost too many friends that day but I haven't been well and I knew I had to come.

We had been sent to make up a Canadian Division. They went in on the first wave. They were mad you know, quite mad. Do you know what they were doing the night before we went in - playing Tarzan, swinging on ropes from trees. There wasn't any sleep for any of us and their officers weren't any better. When we complained to one of them, he went and joined them. We'd been shut in with them for days on end and you never knew what they were going to do next.

We were delayed going in. The Canadians had been delayed, held back so that the incoming tide could add a few more inches so that they would be carried over the obstacles that had been built along the shore. They hadn't expected the tree trunks laced with mines as well as the other obstacles. That was what caught a lot of them out..

It was a long run in and men started being sea sick almost before we left the mother ship. I can't ever remember feeling so ill. I reached the stage where I didn't care about the noise or the shooting or the Germans, all I wanted was to get off that landing craft and get on to firm land. The sea was rough and there were squalls of rain. Then the craft slowed down and the ramps were down and we lined up ready to leave. We'd all been issued with condoms and put them over the end of the rifles to keep them dry and we were pleased we had. I was almost up to my chest in the water, wading towards the shore. We went through hell. Bodies were floating in the sea, being tossed about in the waves so that they looked as though they were swimming and, as they turned over, I saw that they were our own company. These were the Canadians that had been so noisy the previous night. These were men we knew and, although they'd got on our nerves, they were our friends. Some bodies were caught up on the metal traps and wooden obstacles that had been laid and, in that moment, I hated the Nazis.

There were houses along the sea front and they all seemed to be machine gun posts. Gun fire was raking the beaches and we had to make our way through it, through the injured and dead lying on the sand. The beach master was shouting at us to hurry and get in the shelter of the wall. I'll never know how I made it. I leant back against the wall to get my breath and I looked back at a scene I could never have imagined. Other

landing craft were being held back. One of the guns from a battleship
opened up and the houses along the front disappeared.

There were a few snipers, but they were soon dealt with and we were
moving on.

Frank Tasker

In fact, by the time Frank landed, many of the German posts had been
destroyed and the Canadians were dealing with the enemy in the town
itself.. The success on the beach was partly due to the beach master,
Captain Maud, a big, dark, bearded man who roamed the beaches
yielding a cudgel and accompanied by his Alsatian dog. Nobody argued
with Captain Maud.

It was speed and dash that saved many of the Canadians. These were
some of the toughest soldiers in the world and they didn't hang about.
They had come ashore opposite some of the strongest German defences
but, before they could attack them, they had to get across the beach and
they were mined. They dealt with them in the best way they could. They
ran across them. The majority of the Canadians that were killed that day,
were killed on the beaches. Despite all the difficulties they encountered,
they had forced their way seven miles inland before dusk fell.

Some of the officers thought the sea was too rough to launch the
tanks through the sea. Without tank support, the infantry were having a
rough time. There was general relief when the first D.D. (Duplex Drive)
tank emerged on to the beach and shed the protective canvas skirt and
pipes that had allowed it to travel through water. These swimming tanks
were one of General Hobart's inventions and they allowed the tanks to
be launched from some way out. These inventions were called Hobart's
Funnies but they were more than useful on D day. One of the Funnies was
the Flail Tank which dealt with the land mines. The flails rotated in front
of the tank, beating the ground and exploded any mines that they hit. The
infantry could advance safely behind them. There were also the bridging
tanks and the bobbin tanks (the path layers)

I landed on Juno, Red Nan sector, into a hail of machine gun bullets.
When we stopped and dropped the canvas skirt and flotation gear and
they saw we were a Sherman tank, they stood there and stared at us with
their mouths open. I'll never forget the look of astonishment on that group
of German faces. Then I was surprised. There was a mini submarine and

this naval guy standing up through his conning hatch waving me on, They'd cleared a path through the mines and he pointed me towards my target. I found out they'd been waiting submerged for forty eight hours before they had the order to go and clear this path. I was able to swing round and take out my target, a gun emplacement. The houses along the beach were full of machine guns and so were the dunes but I was pleased to see that other tanks were following on behind, mostly D.D.s like myself and some from L.C.T.s

We then moved on to our next target and it wasn't easy driving a tank through these narrow French streets and the French were incredible. There was this battle going on a few hundred yards away from them and they were carrying on life as if we didn't exist. Most of the French were delighted to see us but there were some that supported the Germans. We drove down this road and there was this funny looking truck with a charcoal burner on the running board and a couple of people talking in a doorway. I took off my earphones and asked them in my best French to move the truck out of the way. They didn't budge. They thought we were Tommies but I'm French Canadians and I let them have it in best back street French. They moved quickly enough then and we were through.

Canadian Soldier

....

Each man was carrying enough rations, water and ammunition for 24 hours. Fully equipped, their small packs weighed 27.5 kgms. Each man carried two British Mills 36m hand grenades. These had a delay of four seconds when the pin was withdrawn and weighed 0.7kgms. Many of the experienced men would carry as many grenades as they could manage.

....

We went in at 09.30 hours. We should have gone in at 08.00 hours but the first men to land had been held up on the beaches. There were hundreds of us waiting to go in, we sat there waiting and watching. It was like being at the pictures but this time it was for real. It was difficult to see clearly what was going on on the beaches because of the smoke but we could see the land beyond and we could see around us.

We were at the part of the beach known as La Breche with the 3rd British Infantry Division. I was driving a 15 hundredweight Bedford truck carrying a Bren gun, ammunition and petrol.. Tony Wharf and I sat there completely mesmerised by the scene in front of us. We couldn't take our eyes off it.. We were aware of all the craft around us and the continuous flow of air cover in the sky

As the landing craft approached the beach there was a whistling sound and a bang. Tony and I looked at each other.

"Was that a bullet?" he asked.

"If it was, there'll be a hole," I said.

There was, between the two of us. If it had been six inches to the right, it would have taken my manhood. I got the Bren out of the cab and I would have fired it at the b.....s but the captain stopped me, said I might have hit some of our own troops.

The landing craft took us almost on to the beach and ours was the first vehicle off. We were two wheel drive and our front wheels burrowed into the sand. It was quite steep just there. We got out to see what we could do but the Beach master shouted at us through his loud hailer and told us to leave the truck and get off the beach. They would tow it off. Our officers were in a four wheel drive jeep and they drove straight off. We followed them through to a paddock behind a farm house and dug ourselves in. Then we went back to fetch the truck. As we went down the village street, a French lady caught hold of my sleeve and started saying something I couldn't understand. I followed her back to her home. There was a British officer lying in her garden. I knelt down beside him but he was dead. I reported back to our officer and he said they would get someone to collect and bury him. Then we continued back to the beach. Now we could see it from the other side, see the movement on the sea, see the hundreds of landing craft and the continuous stream of men and traffic making their way across the beach. The tide was out and we could see the obstacles that held up the first troops to land, the rolls of barbed wire and dragons teeth, the mine poles, hedgehog and tetrahedra anti tank obstacles. A lot of them had been pushed to one side and paths made through them. There were flail tanks working along the beaches and broken down vehicles and bodies of dead soldiers. They were being collected and laid out in an open air mortuary. It was absolute chaos but it was organized chaos. There was constant gunfire and bombing and any number of German prisoners being taken back through the village. I was surprised how young they were, hardly out of school, I thought. I was an old man of twenty-one.

We were specialists, engineers, surveyors, building experts. We were the technical unit of the British Third Infantry Division and, although fighting was still going on around us, we started checking public services, reconnecting water supplies and repairing roads.. The local people were wonderful and helped a lot. They did a lot of the work themselves. I had to calculate what supplies were necessary and the pioneers would move the supplies and the equipment.. I was responsible for an area from Arromanches to Hermanville.

Sergeant Jock MacKay told Tony and me that we were needed for a job but wouldn't say what it was. There was a carthorse in the middle of a field and it was in a dreadful state, shivering with his head hanging down. Not far from him, was a dead Frenchman. The poor horse was in shock. Its hooves had been blown off. The field had been mined. We shot the horse. It really upset me shooting the horse, I would rather have shot a German any day. Sergeant MacKay got the Frenchman out and we put up a notice saying unmarked minefield.

Later on, the corporal found a couple of folding bikes, the sort the paras used and he said, "Let's go and shoot a few Germans." We reached some cross-roads and paused to get our bearings when the guns opened up. We were under heavy mortar fire and the target seemed to be those cross roads. We dived into a ditch and it was ages before we could move. As soon as there was a gap in the firing, we got on those bikes and pedalled back to camp at breakneck speed. There had been an emergency, the Germans had broken back towards the coast, and we hadn't been there. I was the more senior of the two and I was put on a charge. I had to see the major and he asked me what I'd been doing and I told him I'd been on reconnaissance.

"What, on a bicycle?" he said.

I didn't hear any more about it. There were other things that took priority.

Eric Saywell - Royal Engineers

Eric Saywell centre. He was the only one of the 3 friends to survive the War.

All the while the lines of landing ships sailed on. In front of us landing craft were being blown up or caught on the beach obstacles and a line of debris and bodies was beginning to darken the tide line but still the lines of landing ships came on, peeling off in smaller groups towards their particular destinations. There was quiet on our craft. Everyone was quiet. There had been jokes when they first left the mother ship but now there was quiet, each man quiet with his own thoughts. Some were quietly being sick into brown paper bags, others sat staring ahead of them. It's strange how emotions hit you at a time like this. I heard a man sobbing and it was as much as I could do to stop sobbing myself. The noise of the shells going overhead disturbed the silence and fountains of water rose into the air alongside us. The wallowing motion of the craft slowed down. We were coming into shallower water. Not a word was said. Men took up their rifles and machine guns. There was the click of bolts being drawn and rammed home. It all seemed to happen in slow motion. The ramp was down and the men were filing out in two lines. They waded through knee deep water. I saw several stagger and fall and I can remember thinking, "You poor bastards."

Marine Davis - Deck hand on L.C.T.

....

The 48th and 41st Commando's target was for each of them to land at either end of the rocky coast line between the two beaches Sword and Juno and meet up by mid-day. The first wave had experienced heavy fire from the German positions and had not been able to clear the beach heads. The Commandos experienced bad landings and, without the aid of their tanks, experienced difficulties they hadn't expected.. The 48th commando was held up by the heavily fortified village of Langrune. Every villa had been turned into a concrete strong point and the roads were blocked by concrete walls, 6 feet high and 5 feet thick. The 41st experienced trouble at Lion sur Mer which the French had told them was deserted but the area to the west of the village was heavily defended. German reinforcements were brought up. The 21st Panzer Armoured Division planned to attack that evening but they were startled by the massive reinforcement for the 6th Parachute Division. All the heavy equipment was towed in by 250 gliders. R.A.F. fighters dived almost to the ground as they machine gunned the anti-aircraft posts. They flew so low that the sky was darkened by them and the noise was so intense that the Germans were disorientated. The Germans believed that they were about to be attacked. By the time they had recovered, the allies had dug themselves in.

. . . .

The first wave had hit Sword beach at 07.25 hours.

We went in at 08.15. It was a long run in and rough too. Then we came on a midget submarine, X23. That was a surprise. He was there to guide us in and we were pleased to see him because with the smoke and dust we couldn't identify our exact position. Then we saw an L.C.T. returning with its ramp jammed half open. There were four of these craft to each beach and each of them carried tanks that worked in groups of three, the centre one carried a 60 foot probe filled with explosive to be pushed through the beach defences. This not only opened up a way through the defences, it also exploded the mines in the immediate area. To see this A.V.R.E. (Armoured Vehicle Royal Engineers) craft returning with her tanks still on board was a blow. It meant we would have to get over the beach the hard way. Our task was to coordinate the opening of the exits from the beach.

. . . .

As we closed on the shore, we saw a line of men lying prone along the water line. As the ramp went down, we saw that they were all dead. A burst of machine gun fire came uncomfortably close. We were wading knee deep through the water. Fortunately there was a lull in the firing and we made a dash for the shelter of a tank. Then the machine gun started up again. It was coming from dead ahead of us and we could make out the silhouette of low fortifications. German stick grenades were thrown over the tank but the sand softened their effect. We were desperately searching for grenades amongst our own equipment when Lieutenant Tony Milne arrived with his machine gun platoon. The 2nd

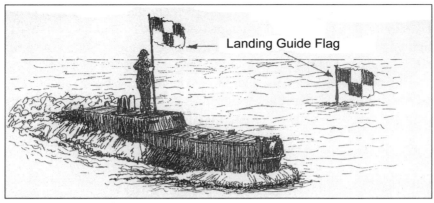

Midget submarines X20 & X23

Battalion Middlesex regiment was equipped with Bren gun carriers carrying Vickers machine guns. The leading carrier drove straight at the German trench line firing the Vickers. There was silence, then fifteen survivors surrendered. Strongpoint COD had been taken.

Officer of 2nd Battalion, Middlesex Regiment

Reinforcements arriving

AVRE - Armoured Vehicle Royal Engineers with a petard mounted on the front

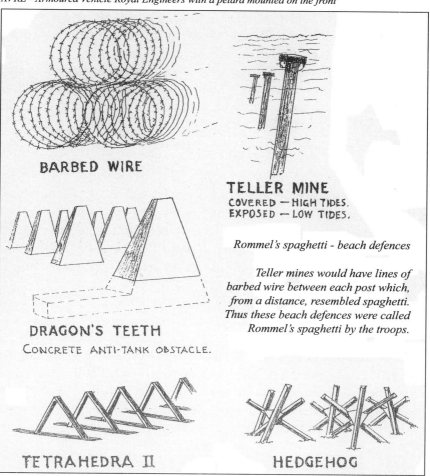

BARBED WIRE

DRAGON'S TEETH

CONCRETE ANTI-TANK OBSTACLE.

TETRAHEDRA II

TELLER MINE

COVERED — HIGH TIDES.
EXPOSED — LOW TIDES.

Rommel's spaghetti - beach defences

Teller mines would have lines of barbed wire between each post which, from a distance, resembled spaghetti. Thus these beach defences were called Rommel's spaghetti by the troops.

HEDGEHOG

Sword beach included Lion sur Mer and Ouistreham at the mouth of the Orne Canal. The Germans had relied on the batteries at Merville and Le Havre to defend this area. Their guns had pointed along the beaches and covered the beach obstacles and gun emplacements in the dunes. There were heavier artillery pieces further inland. Lt. Colonel Otway had taken the Merville Battery but the allies were concerned about Le Havre. The infantry assault teams comprised companies from the South Lancashire Regiment (to land on Peter sector); the Suffolk Regiment (Queen sector) and the East Yorkshire Regiment (Roger Section) with the support of D.D. tanks. They were to open up exits through which the follow up troops, the commandos and more tanks could pass. UDT (Underwater Demolition Teams) units and engineers were to deal with the obstacles. Some of these were frogmen who worked underwater to defuse bombs and booby traps attached to the Tetrahedra. A later landing was to comprise the Lincolnshires, the Royal Norfolk, The King's Own Scottish Borderers, the Royal Ulster rifles, the Royal Warwickshire and the King's Shropshire Light Infantry. H hour was 07.25.

....

I never realized there were so many churches in France. We had been shown maps at the briefings but there were no names on the maps. I picked out a church spire to guide us towards our landing point. As we approached the shore, I could see all these Church spires and I didn't know which was ours so I picked the tallest and told the naval chappie to aim for that.

Captain of the Royal Norfolks

The DD tanks should have landed first but they were slowed down by the tides and the infantry assault teams landed in front of them. Casualties were heavy but the majority made it to the dunes. Then the tanks, Shermans and Churchills emerged from the sea and gave protection to the men crossing the beach.

Two of the tanks went right to the bottom when they were launched and other tank drivers had difficulties. Some of them started floating in circles but they managed to get ashore in a series of circular movements. The sea was rough. We were fighting the sea rather than the enemy. There were only four of nineteen D.D. tanks that made it to the beach. We fired from the water. I was concerned about the men already on the beach but the defences had to be breached. I fired off frigate bombs at the beach obstacles and cleared it for the L.C.T.s to run in and offload the flail tanks. Then we went for the German strongholds. We had petards, mortars, 25lbs explosives that could be fired from 50 yards maximum. They could break up concrete. We also had General Wades, 25 - 30lbs shaped charges which had to be clamped on to the concrete which meant we had to get out of the tanks to use them.

J.H.B. Tank Commander.

I saw a lunatic sight. I rubbed my eyes to make sure I wasn't hallucinating - tanks coming out of the sea, amphibious tanks. This surely was the enemy's secret weapon. It looked as though God and the world had forsaken us.

Lt. Jahnke.

One tank was followed by a bridge-carrying Sherman. A German anti tank gun fired at it so the Sherman drove straight up to it and dropped its bridge directly on to the emplacement, putting the gun out of action. By this time, flail tanks had landed and were busy clearing the beach of mines, flailing right back to below the high water mark. Other tanks used bangalores, snakes or serpents to blow holes through the barbed wire followed by fascine carrying tanks that dropped bundles of wood into anti tank ditches and traps. Bulldozers were also landing and clearing the beach. The troops were held up by the heavy German defence at Lion sur Mer.

Then the second wave came in carrying the commandos. They came in as if it was a Sunday afternoon outing. You could hear them singing rowdy army songs before the ramps went down on their landing craft. Bugles were blowing and Brigadier, the Lord Lovat came wading through the water accompanied by his piper playing a Scottish lament. There was little or no fighting on the beach. Mortars were coming from inland along with shells and sniper fire. The fighting was moving inland.

I splashed out of the water and saw one of Peter's section lying just above the water line and I could see that he was calling out to me, not that I could hear a sound other than the heavy bombardment and the whine and explosions of the gunfire. I bent over him and saw that he had been shot across the legs and I pulled him higher up on to the beach but there was nothing I could do to help him. His legs were almost severed and I knew I couldn't stop any longer. Our orders were not to stop for anything but to get to our target. I had to leave him. I had to push on to the Ouistreham battery and the Casino. That was our objective. I had to turn my back on him but I can still hear him calling after me, "Stop a minute, Sir. For Christ's sake, stop a minute."

Captain Kieller - 10 Commandos

The French commandos landed on Sword, men who had escaped from Dunkirk and were waiting for this moment. They were so impatient to get ashore that some of them jumped into the sea and swam.
Later one of them said:
I cried, not because I was sad but because I was coming home.

....

Our Frenchmen came pouring over the beach, grinning all over their faces and chattering like a lot of sparrows. There was still shooting but they didn't seem to notice. We all queued up and poured out of the same gap as if we were on pay parade.Then as we got to the road, French people began to appear. They seemed to know these were French soldiers and there were flowers and bottles of Calvados. I had a couple of mouthfuls and so did the men. I don't know how the French got on with war with the welcome they were having but we had our target to meet and we left them to it.

Intelligence Officer. No 4 Commandos

4 Commandos - Sword Beach

We got snarled up on the beach. The entrances and beaches hadn't been completely cleared and the landing craft were coming in pretty steadily. We'd got used to queueing up for things back in Britain but we didn't expect to have to queue to get into battle. We let the Commandos through although they were held up for a while. You didn't have to look at their uniforms to know their nationality. The Brits were laid back but there was a look of determination on their faces and you wouldn't have argued with one of them and the French - they all seemed little men and they were excited. They were chattering and they had a similar look of determination on their faces. If we hadn't let them through, they'd have got there. Then there was a group of Poles. They called the Poles lance happy and that was about right. There was no expression on their faces. Their feelings showed in their movements. They were back in Europe and they were going to stay. Who were we to argue with them. They had been shut out of their own country for nearly five years. They were going home.

N.C.O. Royal Engineers

B rigadier Lord Lovat was walking round the assembly area and was perfectly at ease. The noise and shooting didn't seem to bother him. He commanded the 10th Brigade, the inter-allied brigade, including French and Polish commandos under his control

We'd a couple of prisoners with us and Lord Lovat looked across at me and said, "Oh, you're the man with the languages. Ask them where the Howitzers are." So I did but they didn't answer. The men started to gather round him. They were getting angry but I could see from the look on their faces that they didn't know what I was talking about. I took their pay books out of their pockets and discovered that one of them was Polish and the other Russian. We had a Pole in our ranks and I remembered him telling me that they learned French in school, so I spoke to him in my schoolboy French and, immediately, his face lit up and he started to talk. But Lovat spoke a lot better French than I did and he took over.

    The Pole's information was useful and we diverted round a wood to a paved road and we rode our bikes into Colleville sur Mer. It was a mess. People stood in the doorways staring at us taking no heed of the gunfire. A man in a blue smock was pasting up notices saying Invasion and carrying instructions about what to do. As we went by, they seemed to slowly understand who we were. Then they started calling out," Vive les Tommies, Vive La France." We didn't stop. We were expected at Pegasus Bridge.

Corporal No 10 Commando

Lord Lovat's piper, Bill Millin pipes a lament

I was 20 and had volunteered for the Commandos. I was posted to Signal Troop 1st Special Services Brigade (later known as N°1 Brigade) I was a signalman. Our job was to maintain signals between Units 3, 4 and 6 Commandos and N° 45 (Royal Marine) Commandos. Our Brigadier was Lord Lovat. We trained at Petworth in Sussex and then moved to Seaford on the coast near Newhaven, we knew something was in the wind.

Our unit moved into a closed off holding area near Southampton. Thousands of troops were on the move. Security was tight. Our camp was under canvas. All leave was suspended. We were all briefed on the landing areas but there were no names on the maps.

We were driven in trucks to Warsash in Southampton Water on the 5th June. It seemed that all the population of Southampton were lining the streets cheering us on. It was a perfect summer's evening. We embarked and sailed down Southampton Water with people on the banks cheering us on. It was more like a regatta than a prelude to war.

The landing craft was flat bottomed and we felt every wave. I'm a good sailor and I wasn't worried but most of the men were sick, they couldn't wait to get on dry land. The English Channel was full of all types of ship from landing craft to battleships and overhead the continuous drone of aircraft.

Our task was to land on the left flank of Sword Beach and link up with the 6th Airborne. We had to travel 12 miles. Our Brigade was not to get bogged down by heavy fighting. We were to avoid any strongpoints and leave them to the Infantry to mop up.

The rough seas seemed to subside as we ran into the beach. Heavy fire from our battleships was pounding the German defences. Our troop was more excited than nervous. Many of us had not been in action. A few had been on Commando raids. We had a wet landing in 6 feet of water but we all had Mae Wests and floated ashore. We all carried Bergen rucksacks and signals equipment and, of course, our firearms, in my case, a 303.

The assault infantry of 3rd Division had secured the beach.

The beach was very busy with the Beachmaster directing traffic - stores, trucks, jeeps, tanks. Stretcher bearers were collecting bodies and a few shells whistled overhead but my main memory is of a Gaumont British Cameraman filming it all. I never did see the film.

We ran up the beach and across the road. That was when we came under mortar fire. We pushed on through the fields and had to take cover from time to time while N° 6 Commando cleared up the opposition. We reached a small village and French people appeared wanting to give us some wine and Calvados. They seemed to think the war was over for them. We couldn't make them understand that they were in the middle of a battle zone.

A sniper shot at us from a church tower. We took cover and a tank was called up and bang, no sniper, no church tower.

We were making steady progress towards the two bridges over the Orne and Caen Canal which we reached soon after mid-day. Lord Lovat lead us over with his piper in the lead. We crossed a few minutes later but we had to run for it as we came under enemy machine gunfire.

We pushed on and reached our objective, the small French village of Le Plein. We dug in around Brigade H.Q. Most of us got out our rations and made ourselves a meal. We had self heating cans of soup and tins of M2V (meat and vegetables) all very acceptable. It was a lovely but somewhat windy summer's evening. Around six o'clock we heard planes overhead, then there was silence for a few seconds, then a swishing sound and gliders started landing around us. One of them hit a brick wall but the troops seemed OK. These were members of 6th Airborne Division to reinforce their units. They leapt out of their gliders and dashed off towards the bridges. They'd all gone in three minutes. Our chaps were in the gliders in a flash and 'recovered' all sorts of goodies, chocolate, bread etc and a newspaper dated 6th June - D Day - these chaps hadn't left until the afternoon. We also found soft rubber seating which we used to line our trenches - very comfortable. We were good at 'liberating' things.

It was very peaceful, not what we had expected. There was the sound of firing in the distance but that was all. We had achieved complete surprise. Our losses were small just one man wounded. Things became hotter later when the Germans counter attacked but that was all to come. In the meantime we had landed and we had dug in.

N.W. Clark - N.C.O. 1st Commando Brigade Signals

Nobby Clark (right)

Nobby Clark

Commandos come ashore

First of all I went to the Somerset Light Infantry and from there to the Ox and Bucks Light infantry. There were five of us went from our village but I was the only Barnardo's' boy. We used to go back when we had leave and then Mrs Brinsome told me that I would have to pay if I expected to stay there. I can't tell you how hurt I felt, but it was my own fault. I'd looked at her place as home and, of course I didn't have one. I was a lodger. I suppose the army became my life. The men were kind and often asked me home with them. We'd been training for D day for ages and went out from Southampton. We were taken to the docks by lorry and went straight out to the landing craft. There was a storm brewing and those craft were welded or riveted in the middle so that each side seemed to go up independently of each other. I tell you that by the time I got to France, I wasn't sea sick, I was sea drunk. It was ages before I stopped feeling the movement of the waves.

We'd been on those craft the whole weekend, waiting for the weather to ease up. As far as you could see there were other craft and ships with waiting men and equipment. We had six lorries on our craft. The first two were towing six pounder guns. There were five men to each lorry. I was in the first one. There were two medical lorries behind us and, behind them, two ammunition lorries. Then there were the soldiers as well. We had our rations and primus stoves so that we could brew up or we had billy cans with a meths candle in the bottom.

We had been called together early on the morning of June 6th and told that we were going to Northern France and what our duties would be. As it grew light, the whole world seemed to be moving. All the landing craft, all the small boats were moving out to sea, hundreds of them. The naval guns had set up a hell of a barrage. You couldn't hear yourself think, let alone speak. As we were ready to run in, the barrage stopped and we ran right on to the beach. We didn't even get our feet wet. Then the lorry was moving forward. My mate was shot as we were moving off but we couldn't stop for him. There wasn't time. I was in the lorry manning the machine gun. We were moving up the beach. I hadn't been in France more than a quarter of an hour and I got a German bullet in my thigh. The Sergeant pulled the bullet out and rough bandaged the wound. He saw to the manhandling of the gun. The wound hurt but I could live with it. Our job was to defend *the beaches. You must understand, we weren't the first to go in. We were the third wave. The assault infantry had gone in and then the commandos (the green berets) Our job was to defend the beaches, stop the Germans from retaking the beaches.*

I was in the slit trenches for two days. I can't really describe what it was like. There was always noise and movement over the sand.. There were broken down vehicles littering the sand and men lying where they had fallen, not that they were left there for long. The stretcher bearers were working non stop. There was the smoke. We were breathing smoke. The Germans had blown up one of their ammunition dumps. There were the lines of the German prisoners being herded on to the sand waiting for shipment to England and the machine gunfire from the German planes flying over us. Some of the prisoners were shot up by their own planes.

Then I was ordered out. I wanted to stay with the men but all wounded men were ordered out. I was taken off in a DUKW, an amphibious craft. That trip out from the beaches was even worse than the one going in. We were dive bombed and shot at and it wasn't much better when we got on the ship. I went to a military hospital at Halifax. I was there twelve weeks. Then the doctor asked me if I could walk and I said I didn't know. I hadn't tried. The next day, I was sent on a three mile route march and three days later, I was back in France.

Pt. Charles Jeffries. - Ox & Bucks

UTAH

The Americans landed on Utah. The landings had been planned with the same meticulous care as those of the British and Canadian forces. As soon as the naval bombardment ceased at 06.30 hours, DD tanks were to land immediately followed by the assault teams of 2nd Battalion of the 8th Infantry. The second wave of the 2nd Battalion of the 8th Infantry plus combat engineers and demolition teams would land five minutes later. The third wave was to follow fifteen minutes after the first with Sherman and Bulldozer tanks. Two minutes after them detachments of the 237th and 299th Engineer Combat Battalions would land on the beach. It didn't work that way.

Admiral Ramsay had said that assault craft should be launched no more than eight miles out to sea but (the American Admiral) Admiral Kirk was worried about the effect the bombardment would have on his ships and he kept them further out. Most of the men had a run in of eleven and a half miles and, in those seas and the useless nausea pills they had swallowed, many of the men were suffering severe bouts of sea sickness. And the American soldiers had not been issued with the brown paper bags that their allies had.

The Atlantic Wall along Utah beach consisted of 28 batteries strung out along the dunes as well as concrete pillboxes and infantry emplacements. There were also the mines and obstacles that had been built below the low water mark. The land behind the dunes had been flooded for several miles and needed to be crossed by any of the five causeways that lead from the beaches.

The aerial and naval bombardments preceding the landings did not do a lot of damage but they completely demoralized the German troops manning the strongholds. Some of these were recovering from fighting on the Russian Front, others were seventeen year old boys recruited from the Hitler Youth.

The assault craft were to be lead in by four control craft but three of these had been lost on the run in. One was fouled by rope and two

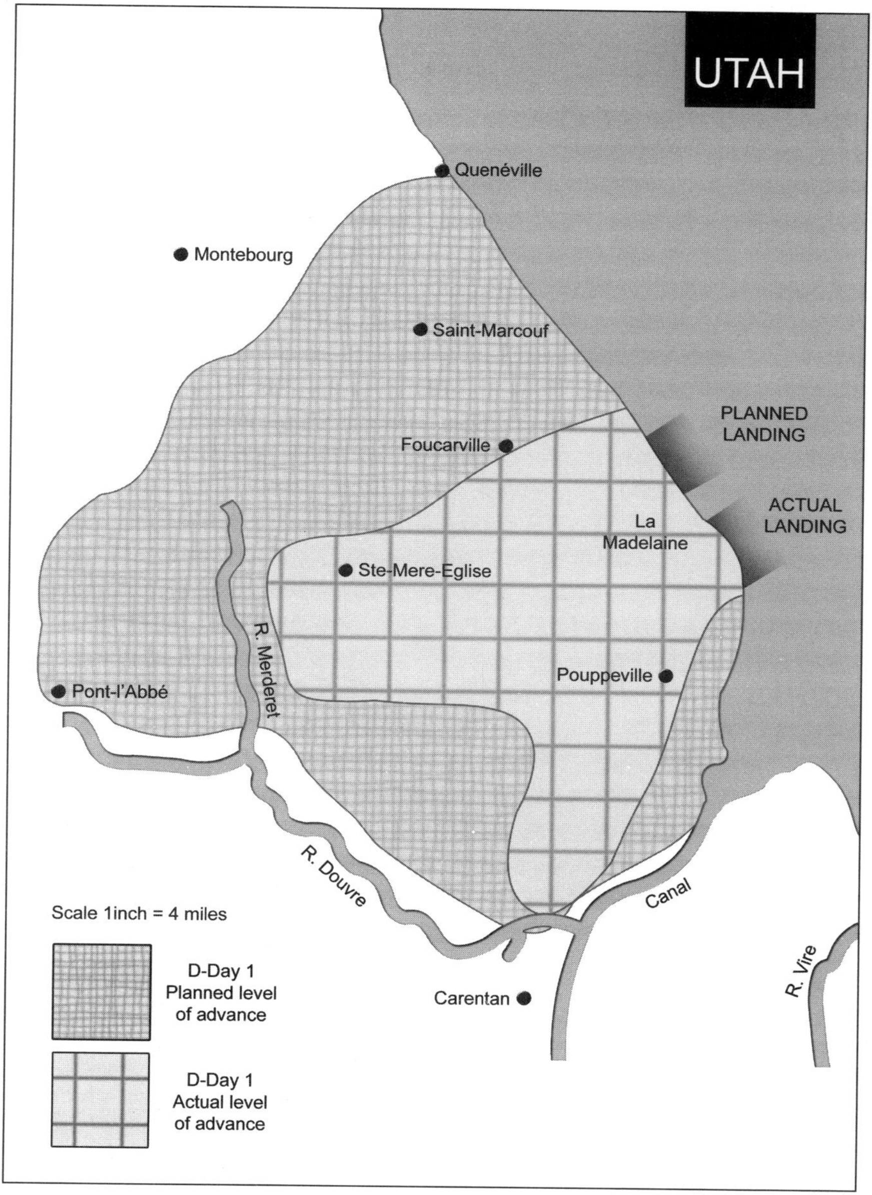
UTAH
Quenéville
Montebourg
Saint-Marcouf
PLANNED
LANDING
Foucarville
ACTUAL
LANDING
La
Madelaine
Ste-Mere-Eglise
R. Merderet
Pouppeville
Pont-l'Abbé
R. Douvre
Canal
Scale 1inch = 4 miles
D-Day 1
Planned level
of advance
Carentan
R. Vire
D-Day 1
Actual level
of advance

Landings at Utah

Moving in: US Troops disembarking at the beach head

hit mines. L.C.T.s were circling looking for directions. Two Naval officers, Lts. Howard Vander Beek and Sims Gauthier realized what was happening, used their bullhorns (loudspeakers) and instructed the craft to follow them in, taking them to within three kilometers of the shore which gave them a shorter run in. As it was, they landed in the wrong place, a mile adrift from their scheduled target. This was caused by the exceptionally strong tidal currents, the waves and too much smoke.

They were lucky. Had they landed at Exit 3, they would have met formidable opposition. The Germans had relied on the flooded area behind the dunes to hold back the enemy so Exit two was not guarded as heavily as the other exits. The men guarding exit 2 were completely traumatized by the bombardment.

....

Brigadier General Theodore Roosevelt was in the first craft to land on the beach and he soon sized up the situation. He was a veteran of fifty seven years and was considered to be too old for the invasion but he had talked his way in to be included claiming that he was needed to steady the boys. He realized that they had landed almost opposite the most southerly causeway and he would need to move all the troops further north to reach their designated venue. He made the most of the situation.

"We'll start the war right here," he said. The only problem he faced was how to direct the following troops to this change of plan but he soon organized that.

German 88mm guns were firing across the beaches and snipers were hidden in the dunes. Tanks attacked the former and the infantry dealt with the latter.

The tanks were firing as they came out of the sea Captain John Ahearn drove through five feet of water in his waterproofed tank. He divided his fourteen tanks into two groups commanding one himself and giving command of the other to Lt Yeoman. Ahearn turned left looking for a gap in the dunes while Yeoman turned right

Wehrmacht Artillery Guarding Beaches

Swimming Tanks - Hobarts funnies turned out to be not so funny for the enemy

Sector	Assault Formation	DD Units	Remarks
UTAH VII US CORPS	4th Inf DIV US with one RCT	70 Tank Bn	30 Tanks launched at 3000 yds 1 foundered

We got through the sea wall and saw a German fortification right in front. We fired the guns and a couple of dozen Wermacht troops emerged, their hands above their heads and began running towards us. I got down to take them prisoners but they signed to me to stay put and started shouting, 'Achtung meinen'. I gestured to them to move across to the road and, taking them prisoners, I handed them over to the infantry, who took them down to the craft on the beach. They weren't German at all but Ost Battalion, troops from Georgia in the Soviet Union.

....

Hundreds of German prisoners were filing down to the beach, most of them dazed by the bombardment and completely overcome by the sheer logistics of the American army.

....

It was a piece of cake. We'd had worse during training. Running into the beaches was a bit grim with the waves and people being sick but then I caught sight of the beach and it was like coming on to our beach back home in Maine.

....

The naval guns had put the fear of God into the Germans. They seemed dazed but we still had some pretty strong pockets of opposition and then they let their secret weapon loose on us. We couldn't believe they were serious, miniature tanks crawling out of the dunes and controlled by wires. They were supposed to be packed with enough explosives to blow up a tank but they never got near one.

....

We went in on Utah Beach at mid-day on June 6th, the only Brits amongst the American troops. It was chaos on the causeway, absolute gridlock but, as soon as we showed our passes personally signed by Eisenhower, gaps were made in the traffic so that our two jeeps and staff car could push through. We were part of the 30th Advanced unit reporting to Naval Intellegence. Our job was to move ahead of the advancing troops and report on targets mainly in the Cherbourg and Brittany areas.

We relied on the French Resistance for information, particularly on the German positions. It was high risk work but exciting and worthwhile.

Commander Patrick D Job

R oosevelt's main problem now, was congestion on the causeway. Queues of vehicles were building up, waiting to move on. In the end he went to the front of the queue and directed the traffic himself. He was everywhere that day, marching up and down the beach with his walking stick, oblivious of any danger.

"For Christ's sake get that crazy chap under cover," one of the officers called out. "He's going to get himself killed.," It was pointed out that he was the General.

We had almost crossed the causeway when I thought I saw two helmets dodge behind some bushes so I told the major. He asked if they were German or American and I said I hadn't seen. "Don't want to shoot our own chaps," he said. So he let off a yellow flare and these two men stood up and we could see they were American then and they had the eagle badge on their uniforms. When the major told them who we were, they said that they were sure pleased to see us and so would General Taylor be. They had been sent to guide them in to Poupeville where he was waiting. We had joined up with him by mid day.

Colonel Russell Reeder, C.O. of the 12th Infantry, landed on Utah at 10.30 hours and realized that they had landed in the wrong place but took a similar attitude to Roosevelt that they would use that causeway.

He was met by Roosevelt who shouted at him to look at the line of jeeps and not a wheel moving. Reeder quickly sized up the situation. "Right," he said, "we're going through the flooded area."

Aerial reconnaissance had said that the water was little more than ankle deep. They got it wrong. In some places the water was waist high and in the irrigation ditches, it was over their heads.. They had to make their way through this for more than two kilometers.. It took them nearly four hours. The 12th Infantry reached its D day Objective and took up position at Les Forges, sending a reconassaince platoon to establish contact with the 82nd Airborne. By late afternoon, the 8th infantry and its supporting regiment, the 22nd had met up with the 82nd Airborne at St Martin de Varreville and St Germain de Varreville, somewhat short of their objective but well established and pleased to be inland. Reinforcements were pouring in. Casualties had been remarkably light, mostly caused by mines. The Americans rested, ready to push on into the Cotentin Peninsula and Cherbourg.

Omaha

The 2nd and 3rd Battalions disembarked from the U.S.S. Henrica and H.M.S. Empire Anvil at 03.45 hours to assault Omaha north of Colleville at 06.30 hours. Rommel had always said that the Allies could only be defeated on the beaches. The Germans nearly did just that at Omaha. Omaha is a 4 mile crescent of beach with high cliffs at each end and hills in the centre. The area behind was wooded. The Atlantic wall was particularly strong here with eight concrete bunkers housing big guns and pill boxes with anti aircraft guns as well as fortified machine gun points. Intense enemy fire, underwater obstacles and heavy seas caused high casualties before the troops reached the shore. The 2nd Battalion was pinned down on the beach by extremely heavy fire from concrete fortifications, machine gun emplacements and sniper activity. These remained intact despite heavy aerial and naval bombardment.

Omaha was more exposed than Utah and the water rougher. New assaults were to come in every ten minutes until 09.30 hours. The beaches were split into six sections, code named Dog Green, Dog White, Dog Red, Easy Green, Easy Red and Fox Green. The troops that went in on D day were all hardened soldiers. The task of attacking at Omaha had been given to the 1st. U.S. Army Division, America's toughest troops.

The Americans had not expected much opposition but luck was against them. The German 352nd Division, which contained some of their toughest troops, happened to be on an exercise in the area on counter attack practice. The American landing craft had a run in of twelve miles, many were blown off course by high winds and strong currents. The Germans held their fire until the troops were approaching and landing on the beaches, then they opened up.

OMAHA V US CORPS	1 Inf FDIV US with two RCTs up	743 Tank Bn 741 Tank Bn	Not launched; all beached direct from LCsT 29 Tanks launched at 6000 yds: 27 foundered 2 swam in. 3 beached from LCsT

The bombardment as we went in was terrific. There was no chance of talking to the guy next to you, not that we wanted to. We could see the flashes and the fires and, as it grew lighter, we could see and smell smoke, smoke rising in plumes into the early morning sky and smoke covering the beaches in front of us. We knew there was a smoke screen laid on the

DD Sherman Tank advance, through French streets

beaches but we hadn't expected anything as heavy as this and all the time there was the noise, the aeroplanes overhead and the ships firing their big guns and the rocket ships, it was enough to send you off your mind. There was one chap who did seem gone. He didn't know where he was. All the men were being sea sick, the waves were that rough. The floor was awash with vomit and all the time there was the noise. The chap beside me leaned over and said, 'We're giving them hell. There won't be a German alive by the time we land.' He couldn't have been more wrong.

The eight battalions in the first wave landed on time, despite the bad weather. Fourteen frogmen teams went into the water to deal with the obstacles. They had planned to demolish these before the next wave landed.

The men knew they would be in for a tough fight. Surveillance had told them that the beaches and exits from it would be heavily guarded. The Germans had failed to respond to the naval barrage and the soldiers had been lulled into a false idea of their numbers and strength. They held their fire until the L.C.T.s were close to the beaches and the men were beginning to land before they opened fire and it was deadly. Soldiers were

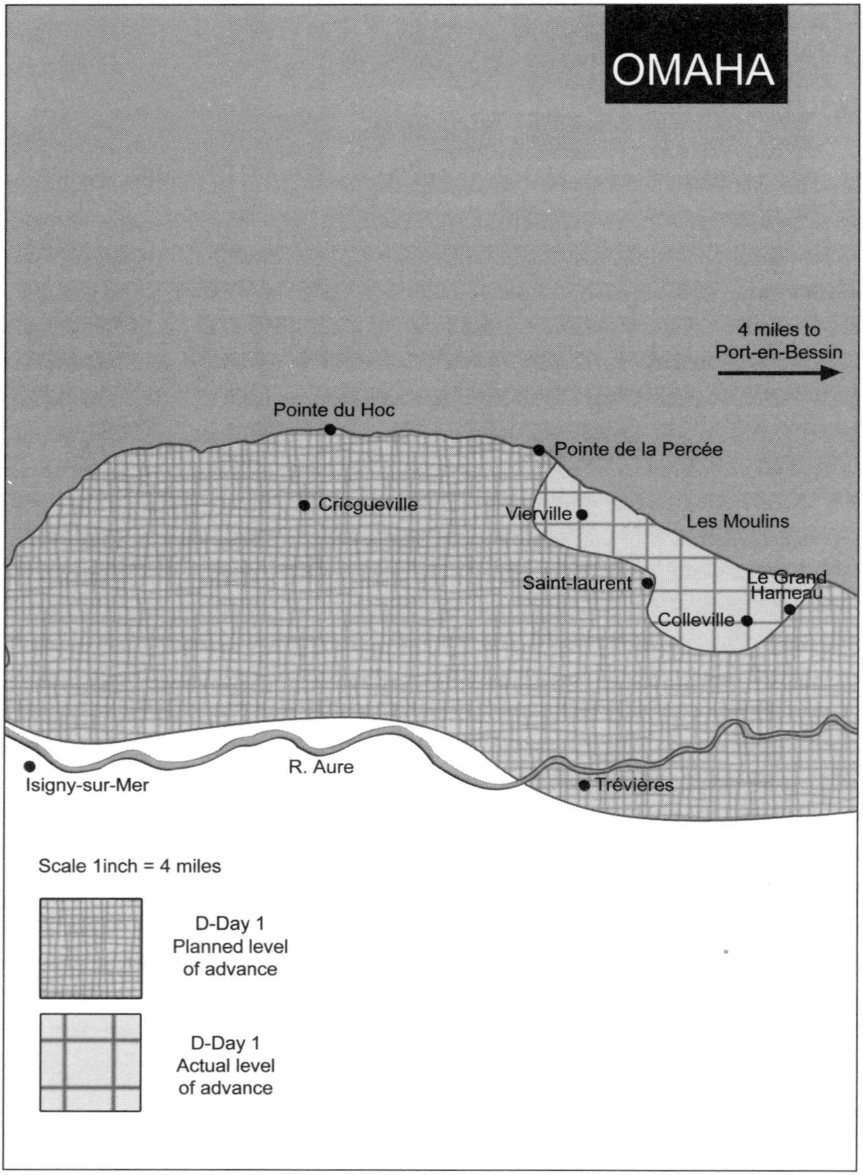
OMAHA
4 miles to
Port-en-Bessin
Pointe du Hoc
Pointe de la Percée
Cricgueville
Vierville
Les Moulins
Saint-laurent
Le Grand
Hameau
Colleville
R. Aure
Isigny-sur-Mer
Trévières
Scale 1inch = 4 miles
D-Day 1
Planned level
of advance
D-Day 1
Actual level
of advance

falling into the water. Landing craft were exploding before the soldiers disembarked. Many of the men decided the only safe way to reach the beach was to dive into the water and swim but they still had to cross the strand. They had to rush the sea wall and they were under fire all the way.

We couldn't stop to help the wounded men but there was one man caught in the surf and I stopped a second to pull him up out of the water before I went on. Tanks were beginning to come out of the water but they were hampered by the obstacles on the approach to the beach and there were abandoned and burning landing craft holding them up. Three tanks had their lids closed and the first one started to run over wounded men. One of the officers had to throw a grenade at him, broke his track. That woke him up.

....

I lost my medic, before we hit the beach, and my radio man had both his legs shot off. What could I do. I was the sergeant and we had a job to do.

....

When we got inland, we found civilians there and some of them were carrying on as they did every day, even some of the shops were open and the fighting was going on all around them. I felt sorry for the French people. They did not seem to understand what was happening and there was so much damage. Whole streets were reduced to rubble.

The Americans had refused the use of Hobart's Funnies save for a limited number of DD tanks. They were relying on the speed, experience and nerve of their own fighting men. Unfortunately intelligence failed to tell the Commander that the 352nd Division of the Panzers had moved into the Omaha area for a night exercise until it was too late.

Omaha was a crescent shaped beach with a shingle bank that was too steep for tanks. There was a concrete wall behind this bank. And along this whole area were gun emplacements, concrete bunkers, pill boxes, fortified machine gun nests and well hidden snipers. The Americans were met by a storm of gunfire. They didn't stand a chance. Men were being shot before they left the landing craft and the demolition teams were being targeted so that they could not make the area safe for the second wave coming in. The troops lacked heavy guns and tanks. It had been left to the officers to decide when they sent in the DD tanks. They were not launched for hours in one area because the Commander considered that the sea was too rough. On the Easy Red beach, only five of thirty two tanks reached the beach.

I was in the 741st tank battalion, commander in charge of a DD tank to land in OMAHA. There was no problem with launching but it was a long way in and the waves grew bigger and the tank began to roll. It started to get so bad I called the men to the turret so they'd have a chance to get out of the tank if it did roll over. Just the driver stayed in position and he was having a bad time. There was a strong current pushing us to the right and a very strong wind whipping up the waves and the bottom of the tank was swilling with sea water.

We were making headway and were within sight of the beach when the engine stopped. I told the men to get out and swim for it. I can't tell you how deflated I felt. I thought we'd let the infantry down. If only they'd launched us a bit nearer the coast we'd have made it. It didn't help when I found out later that of the 29 DD tanks launched, only two had made it to the beach.

Pat Hemery

Some had been launched four miles out and had been swamped or wrecked. In addition to this a lot of equipment was lost in the heavy surf. Many of the men escaped the bullets only to be blown up by mines. The following waves coming in were met by bodies and wounded men being tossed about in the surf and beyond them more fallen soldiers and still the landing craft came bringing more and more men. Some did manage to make their way through the mines and soon the narrow strip of land against the wall, the only place where they were safe from the devastating German fire was crowded with sheltering men.

The situation looked so bad on Omaha that Bradley thought about evacuating the troops but, by the time Montgomery received his signal, things were beginning to improve.

At 13.30. hours the signal was received saying that the troops formerly pinned down on Easy Red, Easy Green and Fox Red beaches were now advancing up the hills behind the beaches. The Commanders were reorganizing the men. They found that in a number of cases, the men were being lead by N.C.O.s, so many of the officers having been killed. On the beaches the medics were helping the injured. Gunfire was still holding them up but a breakthrough had been made. Within half an hour, an attack was launched. Gaps were opened in the wire and men crept across the minefields. At the western end of the beach, three DD tanks were firing at the German gun emplacements giving the infantry a chance to advance and destroy them. Colonel Taylor lead the way across the minefield. He realized the tide was turning in their favour and said to the men around him, "Two kinds of people are staying on this beach, the dead and those that are going to die. Let's get the hell out of here."

They moved on.

While the battle for Omaha was proceeding, an assault on Pointe du Hoc was being made by a force of U.S. Rangers under Colonel Rudder. A German gun emplacement was at the top of the cliffs at this point overlooking the beaches on which the allies were to land. It was essential that these guns were silenced. The exercise was almost impossible with sheer cliffs rising out of the sea and the narrowest of beaches revealed at low tide. RAF bombers had bombed the whole coastal area before the first men landed on the beaches.

....

I was the rear gunner on a Lancaster flying out of Elsham Wolds. Our target was to bomb the Pointe du Hoc. We went in low to make sure of the target. As we turned for home I could see the first of the landing craft making for the shore. We were flying over ships of every shape and size, hundreds of them. I could see everything clearly, the barrage balloons, the puffs of smoke as the naval guns were fired and thick black smoke from burning targets on land, but the only sound I could hear was from our own engines.

The Yanks said we hadn't bombed accurately, blamed us for the problems at Point du Hoc. I went there as soon as I could. We had bombed right on target. You only have to look at the bomb craters to see that.

Geoff Gilbert - sergeant rear gunner RAF

Naval guns had bombarded the gun emplacement but had stopped firing as the Rangers approached. This allowed the Germans to return to the site and, when the Rangers landed, they were waiting for them with machine guns, rifles and grenades. Many were killed or wounded and the survivors found themselves pinned beneath the cliffs. Attempts to scale the cliffs were foiled by the Germans who would wait until men were half way up the rope ladders before they cut them loose and all the time, they were dropping grenades on to them. Men were being shot to pieces and the surf was running red with blood. It seemed a hopeless task.

A destroyer came in and bombarded the emplacement and displaced rocks fell on us that were sheltering under the cliffs but there was a lull in the shooting above us. We had been lobbing grenades at the cliff, making chimneys. We didn't wait. We started up these instead. The Germans surrendered. They had no more fight left in them. They weren't much more than kids, some of them. Talk about a let down. There weren't any guns there, just a couple of tree trunks sticking out where the guns had been. We'd left all our dead and wounded men on the beach for that. If you could have seen the look on the Colonel's face but he sent a reconnaissance party inland and they discovered that the guns had been moved further back from the cliffs. We didn't need any second invitation. We moved in on them. I can tell you, we weren't rangers for nothing. We would have taken anyone and anything the mood we were in."

Soldier of the 5th American Rangers.

Expanding the Beach Head

The objective for the 3rd British Division was to reach Caen by nightfall and either capture it or effectively mask it. They nearly made it. General Montgomery had been doubtful that the target could be achieved because the parachute landings would have given the Germans early warning and time to prepare their defence. To allow the soldiers time to reach the city they needed to clear the beaches and move inland quickly. It was also essential for the beaches to be cleared to allow supplies and equipment easy access. They ran into trouble from the beginning.

German defences were particularly strong on Sword Beach. The three miles behind the road that ran from Riva Bella to Lion sur Mer were impassable. Each of the villas along that stretch had been turned into mini fortresses and each one had to be made safe before the soldiers could advance. Behind the road, there was an area of marsh that had been heavily mined. The beach itself had particularly formidable traps in the form of tetrahedrons and mined stakes that had been difficult to move and the navy had difficulty to get ashore. The beach area was in easy reach of the German coastal artillery with the 11 and 16 inch guns at Le Havre being particularly deadly. Added to this was the beach itself which was very narrow at high tide. Men and machines were getting bogged down, queuing up to get off the beach, sitting ducks for the Germans. It was so bad at one point that the landing craft were held back to allow organization on the beach. Disaster was avoided by the sheer professionalism, training and leadership of the troops. The 3rd Division had cleared the beaches and were moving inland almost on time.

The East Yorks were experiencing difficulties among the Riva Bella barricades. While the South Lancashires with their tanks had covered one and a half miles and were already entering Hermanville, the reserve battalion, the 1st Suffolks were assembling on the outskirts of Hermanville preparing to attack Colleville sur Orne.

No 4 Commando was making rapid progress through Ouistreham lead by a troop of Free Frenchmen with an enthusiasm that only the French can show. They had come home and they were there to stay.

Some of their exploits have become legend*. No 6 Commandos were already pushing up through Ouistreham and Colleville to relieve the men on the Orne Bridges. The 76th Field Regiment had come ashore immediately behind the Suffolks and set up two of their guns on the beach itself.

The real problem was the congestion on the beach but, despite that, the 185th Brigade was assembling inland by 11 o'clock that morning.

The Suffolks successfully overran the two fortified battery positions, code named Hillman and Morris.

We set up the guns on Morris and the garrison started to surrender as soon as the first shot had been fired. They were completely demoralized. The naval bombardment had scared them silly and they came out dazed and not really knowing what was happening. They had no fight left in them. Some of them were only kids. We sent them back down the line and turned our attention on Hillman. We thought it was going to be easy. One platoon had gone forward and taken some prisoners when the battery started up and they had to withdraw. The officers set up a plan. Tanks were brought in and the artillery set up. Then we went in. They tried to fight it out in the galleries and in the shelters. We took fifty prisoners and killed a lot more. We were pleased with ourselves. That battery had been causing our men a lot of trouble.

The Kings Shropshire Light Infantry was primed to make the dash for Caen with the tanks of the Staffordshire Yeomanry but the tanks were held up on the beach. There were rumours that German tanks were advancing and the Brigadier was reluctant to send his men forward without tank support. The Kings Shropshire L.I. set out at mid-day and nearly made it to Caen. By four o'clock when the tanks had caught up with them, they were two and half miles from Caen but they were on their own and had received information that 24 German Mark IV tanks were bearing down on them. The German attack was doomed because it lacked infantry support but their attack was enough to slow the allied attack on Caen.

They may not have captured Caen but they had achieved everything else that was expected of them. The Germans had to move

*Three of them accompanied me along the route they had taken more than fifty years earlier, showing me the exact spot where one of them had been wounded and where their officer had been killed. Their enthusiasm had not waned with the passing years.

their armour to guard the city thus giving the allies time to consolidate the areas they had taken during the day. They had accomplished their initial task.

The 1st Corps assault had been complicated in that it had gone in on two fronts, Juno and Sword Beaches. The 3rd Canadian Division and the 2nd Canadian brigade had been given the most ambitious objective of the day, to advance eleven miles inland and capture Carpiquet Airfield. Despite all the difficulties they encountered, they had advanced seven miles by the time darkness fell. At one time, their tanks had crossed the Caen to Bayeux Road. It was on the actual dash across the beaches that the Canadians had suffered their greatest loss, the Queen's Own Rifles losing fifty per cent of their men as they came in near Bernieres. They only survived because an anti-aircraft ship came close inshore and pounded the German strongholds. There was nothing to stop them then and the reserve battalion that followed them in, The Regiment de la Chaudiere found the beach clear except for a few German snipers and they soon dealt with them. Away to their right, the Royal Winnipeg Rifles and the Regina Rifles had also experienced difficulties on the beach but in less than an hour they had organized themselves and were fighting their way out of Courseilles, almost a mile inland. It took them two hours of heavy house to house fighting. By mid morning, they were two miles inland expecting their reserve battalion to catch up and relieve them but, although they had landed punctually, they were held up in the congestion on the beach and the advance was delayed.

All the same, the Canadians had made spectacular advances by the end of the first day. They had advanced seven miles inland and were threatening Caen from the west. They had linked up with the 50th Division and established a solid beach head up to six miles deep and twelve miles along the coast. They failed to take Carpiquet Airfield. It proved a difficult objective. It was situated on a plateau which gave the Germans a good vantage point and it was strongly fortified with underground shelters and heavy guns. It was a month before the Canadians finally took it after hand to hand fighting.

....

The Hampshires hit problems on Gold Beach. The Beach was covered by gun emplacements but the Germans had expected the allies to invade at high tide and had sited their guns so that they covered the beach above the high water mark. There were high banks between the beach and the road. The two leading companies had got across the beach without much trouble and had by-passed the villages but the Hampshires that followed were caught in the crossfire by the German 352nd Division at the heavily fortified Village of Le Hamel. They were held up there most of the day but they drew the enemy fire and allowed the troops on either side of them a clear run. The Dorsets to their left had no problems and the whole battalion was clear of the beach within forty minutes leaving the 'funnies' to get to work, smashing holes through the concrete walls allowing easy access, breaching minefields and laying tracks over soft spots. The beaches were ready for those who were to follow. It was four o'clock before the Hampshires moved on.

It was much the same on the other section of the beach. La Riviere held up the East Yorks for two hours before they broke through. The 6th Green Howards had an easy passage in comparison and within two hours of landing were settled in on a ridge a mile inland. while the 7th Green Howards were forming up with their tanks to push inland. By nightfall, the Brigade was six miles inland, had already linked up with the Canadians and was only a mile short of the main road between Caen and Bayeux.

The 50th Division, the Desert Rats of 7th Armoured Division who were the most battle experienced troops to land didn't give the Germans a chance once they had gained the initiative on the beaches. By 11 o'clock obstacles had been cleared enough to allow a clear run in for landing craft. Three miles of beach had been cleared of mines and booby traps and ways across the sand had been cleared. The two Brigades coming in later were able to assemble beyond the dunes and marshy area and move inland, not giving the enemy a chance to reorganize. By night time, they had the Bayeux to Caen Road under fire and some men were already in the outskirts of Bayeux which they took next morning.

The 47th Royal Marine Commandos landed east of Le Hamel having taken a terrible battering from heavy gunfire and submerged beach obstacles. Many had lost their weapons but the survivors pressed on with their objective to make their way beyond the beaches and capture the port of Port-en-Bessin where they were to meet up with men of the American 1st Division. They reached the hill overlooking the port but had to wait until reinforcements caught up with them. They duly finished the job on the morning of the 8th.

By midnight the 50th Division had accomplished everything that had been expected of them. They had captured the little port of Arromanches, allowing the construction of the Mulberry Harbour to start straight away. They had cleared a beach head and established a beach organization which allowed troops and equipment to be brought ashore and they had cut the main road behind the beaches.

By dawn on June 6th 1944, 18,000 American and British parachutists were on the ground in Normandy. By midnight, 155,000 allied troops and 10,000 vehicles had landed in France. 4,000 ships had been involved as well as landing craft. By D day 12, 700,000 men had landed, 100,000 vehicles and 600,000 tons of supplies.

....

Skirts lowered these DD Shermans proceeded on convoy from the Beach head

Also...

On June 6th., 1944, Germans on Crete took 400 Greek hostages, 300 Italian Prisoners of War and 260 Jews a hundred miles out into the Mediterranean and scuttled the ship. There were no survivors..

On June 7th. A German Waffen S.S. unit captured 34 Canadians near the villages of Authie and Buron and bayoneted or shot them to death. 43 more wounded Canadian prisoners were killed in a similar way on the orders of the S.S. commanding officer, Lt- Colonel Kurt Meyer.

On that same day the S.S. Das Reich Division carried out reprisals against civilians in the town of Tulle for acts of sabotage by French resistance fighters.
I returned from shopping and found my son and husband hanging from our balcony. What more can I say.
Women and children had been driven from the homes and forced to watch the men being strung up.

Also on that day two trains carrying Hungarian Jews reached Auschwitz. Men were separated from the women and children who were immediately taken to the gas chambers.

Auschwitz Oven

Land Forces Casualties
June 6th - June 30th 1944

British and Canadian troops - 3,356 killed, 15,815 wounded, 5,527 missing.

U.S.army - 5,113 killed 26,538 wounded, 5,385 missing.

German casualties - estimated 80,367 of which 40,526 were P.O.W.s

Air Force Casualties
6 June - 30 August 1944.

R.A.F. Tactical Air Force and Air Defence - 1,036 killed or missing. 829 Aircraft lost

R.A.F. Bomber Command - 6,761 killed or missing. 983 Aircraft lost.

R.A.F. Coastal Command - 382 killed or missing. 224 Aircraft lost

U.S.8th Air Force - 7,167 killed or missing 1,168 Aircraft lost.

U.S. 9th Air Force - 1,369 killed or missing. 897 Aircraft lost.

AIRBORNE FORCES

6th Airborne Division 3rd Parachute Bde- 8th and 9th Bns. The Parachute Regiment
1st Canadian Parachute Bn.
5th Parachute Bde - 7th.,12th and 13th Bns.
The Parachute Regiment 6th Airlanding Bde 12th Bt. The Devonshire Regiment
2nd Bn. The Oxfordshire and Buckinghamshire Light Infantry.
1st Bn The Royal Ulster Rifles.
Divisional Troops 6th airborne Armoured Reconnaissance Regiment R.A.C.
6th Airborne Div Engineers
53rd Airlanding Light Regt. R.A.
6th Airborne Div. Signals.`
U.S. 101st and 82nd Airborne Divisions.

Glider Number 1 – Target: The Caen Canal Bridge

Rank	Name	Serving in ...	Coy/Platoon	Serving as ...
S/Sgt	Wallwork	Glider Pilot Rgmt		Horsa Pilot
S/Sgt	Ainsworth	Glider Pilot Rgmt		Horsa Co-Pilot
W/Cdr	Duder	RAF		Tug Pilot
Lt.	Brotheridge	2nd Oxf.Bucks	D 25	Platoon Cdr
Sgt	Ollis	2nd Oxf.Bucks	D 25	
Cpl	Caine	2nd Oxf.Bucks	D 25	
Cpl	Webb	2nd Oxf.Bucks	D 25	
Cpl	Bailey	2nd Oxf.Bucks	D 25	
L/C	Packwood	2nd Oxf.Bucks	D 25	
L/C	Minns	2nd Oxf.Bucks	D 25	
Pte	Baalam	2nd Oxf.Bucks	D 25	
Pte	Bates	2nd Oxf.Bucks	D 25	
Pte	Bourlet	2nd Oxf.Bucks	D 25	
Pte	Chamberlain	2nd Oxf.Bucks	D 25	
Pte	Edwards	2nd Oxf.Bucks	D 25	
Pte	Gray	2nd Oxf.Bucks	D 25	
Pte	O'Donnell	2nd Oxf.Bucks	D 25	
Pte	Parr	2nd Oxf.Bucks	D 25	
Pte	Tilbury	2nd Oxf.Bucks	D 25	
Pte	Watson	2nd Oxf.Bucks	D 25	
Pte	White	2nd Oxf.Bucks	D 25	
Pte	Windsor	2nd Oxf.Bucks	D 25	
Pte	Jackson 08	2nd Oxf.Bucks	D 25	
Major	Howard	2nd Oxf.Bucks	Officer Commanding Coup de Main Force	
Cpl	Tappenden	2nd Oxf.Bucks	Wireless Operator, Coy. HQ	
Cpl	Watson	Royal Engineers		
Spr	Danson	Royal Engineers		
Spr	Ramsey	Royal Engineers		
Spr	Wheeler	Royal Engineers		
Spr	Yates	Royal Engineers		

Glider Number 1, together with gliders 2 and 3, landed very close to its target, the Caen canal bridge, now named Pegasus Bridge. All three gliders landed within a few minutes of each other.

Glider Number 2 – Target: The Caen Canal Bridge.

Rank	Name	Serving in ...	Coy/Platoon	Serving as ...
S/Sgt	Boland	Glider Pilot Rgmt		Horsa Pilot
S/Sgt	Hobbs	Glider Pilot Rgmt		Horsa Co-Pilot
WO	Berry	RAF		Tug Pilot
Lt.	Wood	2nd Oxf.Bucks	D 24	Platoon Cdr
Sgt	Leather	2nd Oxf.Bucks	D 24	
Cpl	Godbold	2nd Oxf.Bucks	D 24	
Cpl	Cowperthwaite	2nd Oxf.Bucks	D 24	
Cpl	Ilsley	2nd Oxf.Bucks	D 24	
L/C	Roberts	2nd Oxf.Bucks	D 24	
L/C	Drew	2nd Oxf.Bucks	D 24	
Pte	Chatfield	2nd Oxf.Bucks	D 24	
Pte	Lewis	2nd Oxf.Bucks	D 24	
Pte	Cheesley	2nd Oxf.Bucks	D 24	
Pte	Waters	2nd Oxf.Bucks	D 24	
Pte	Clarke 33	2nd Oxf.Bucks	D 24	
Pte	Musty	2nd Oxf.Bucks	D 24	
Pte	Dancey	2nd Oxf.Bucks	D 24	
Pte	Harman	2nd Oxf.Bucks	D 24	
Pte	Warmington	2nd Oxf.Bucks	D 24	
Pte	Leonard	2nd Oxf.Bucks	D 24	
Pte	Weaver	2nd Oxf.Bucks	D 24	
Pte	Radford	2nd Oxf.Bucks	D 24	
Pte	Clark 48	2nd Oxf.Bucks	D 24	
Pte	Pepperall	2nd Oxf.Bucks	D 24	
Pte	Malpas	2nd Oxf.Bucks	D 24	
L/C	Harris	RAMC		Medic
A/Capt	Neilson	Royal Engineers		
Spr	Conley	Royal Engineers		
Spr	Lockhart	Royal Engineers		
Spr	Shorey	Royal Engineers		
Spr	Haslett	Royal Engineers		

Glider Number 2, together with gliders 1 and 3, landed very close to its target, the Caen canal bridge, now named Pegasus Bridge. All three gliders landed within a few minutes of each other.

Glider Number 3 – Target: The Caen Canal Bridge

Rank	Name	Serving in . . .	Coy/Platoon	Serving as . . .
S/Sgt	Barkway	Glider Pilot Rgmt		Horsa Pilot
S/Sgt	Boyle	Glider Pilot Rgmt		Horsa Co-Pilot
WO	Herman	RAF		Tug Pilot
Lt.	Smith	2nd Oxf Bucks	B 14	Platoon Cdr
Sgt	Harrison	2nd Oxf Bucks	B 14	
Cpl	Higgs	2nd Oxf Bucks	B 14	
Cpl	Evans	2nd Oxf Bucks	B 14	
Cpl	Aris	2nd Oxf Bucks	B 14	
L/C	Madge	2nd Oxf Bucks	B 14	
L/C	Cohen	2nd Oxf Bucks	B 14	
L/C	Greenhalgh	2nd Oxf Bucks	B 14	
Pte	Wilson	2nd Oxf Bucks	B 14	
Pte	Hook	2nd Oxf Bucks	B 14	
Pte	Stewart	2nd Oxf Bucks	B 14	
Pte	Keane	2nd Oxf Bucks	B 14	
Pte	Noble	2nd Oxf Bucks	B 14	
Pte	Crocker	2nd Oxf Bucks	B 14	
Pte	Basham	2nd Oxf Bucks	B 14	
Pte	Watts	2nd Oxf Bucks	B 14	
Pte	Anton	2nd Oxf Bucks	B 14	
Pte	Tibbs	2nd Oxf Bucks	B 14	
Pte	Slade	2nd Oxf Bucks	B 14	
Pte	Burns	2nd Oxf Bucks	B 14	
Pte	Turner	2nd Oxf Bucks	B 14	
Pte	Golden	2nd Oxf Bucks	B 14	
Major	Jacob-Vaughan	RAMC		Medical Officer
L/C	Waring	Royal Engineers		
Spr	Clarke	Royal Engineers		
Spr	Fleming	Royal Engineers		
Spr	Green	Royal Engineers		
Spr	Preece	Royal Engineers		

Glider Number 4 – Target: The Orne River Bridge.

Rank	Name	Serving in . . .		Coy/Platoon	Serving as . . .
S/Sgt	Lawrence	Glider Pilot Rgmt			Horsa Pilot
S//Sgt	Shorter	Glider Pilot Rgmt			Horsa Co-Pilot
F/O	Clapperton	RAF			Tug Pilot
Lt	Hooper	2nd Oxf. Bucks	D 22		Platoon Cdr
Sgt	Barwick	2nd Oxf.Bucks	D 22		
Cpl	Goodsir	2nd Oxf.Bucks	D 22		
Cpl	Reynolds	2nd Oxf.Bucks	D 22		
L/Sgt	Rayner	2nd Oxf.Bucks	D 22		
Cpl	Ambrose	2nd Oxf.Bucks	D 22		
Cpl	Hunt	2nd Oxf.Bucks	D 22		
Pte	Allwood	2nd Oxf.Bucks	D 22		
Pte	Wilson	2nd Oxf.Bucks	D 22		
Pte	Hedges	2nd Oxf.Bucks	D 22		
Pte	Everett	2nd Oxf.Bucks	D 22		
Pte	St. Clair	2nd Oxf.Bucks	D 22		
Pte	Waite	2nd Oxf.Bucks	D 22		
Pte	Clive.	2nd Oxf.Bucks	D 22		
Pte	Timms	2nd Oxf.Bucks	D 22		
Pte	Whitford	2nd Oxf.Bucks	D 22		
Pte	Johnson	2nd Oxf.Bucks	D 22		
Pte	Lathbury	2nd Oxf.Bucks	D 22		
Pte	Hammond	2nd Oxf.Bucks	D 22		
Pte	Gardner 08	2nd Oxf.Bucks	D 22		
Pte	Jeffrey	2nd Oxf.Bucks	D HQ		
Capt	Priday	2nd Oxf.Bucks	D HQ		Coy. 2nd in Command
L/C	Lambley	2nd Oxf.Bucks	D 22		Coy. Clerk
L/Sgt	Brown	Royal Engineers			
Spr	Deighton	Royal Engineers			
Spr	Guest	Royal Engineers			
Spr	Paget	Royal Engineers			
Spr	Roberts	Royal Engineers			

Glider Number 4 was scheduled to land first, but was pulled off course by its tug aircraft and landed by a bridge over the River Dives some 8 miles to the east. Although losing some men in skirmishes along the way, the crew and airborne infantry and engineers successfully fought their way through the flooded Dives valley and back to Hérouvillette, to rendezvous with the Regiment on 7 June.

Glider Number 5 – Target: The Orne River Bridge.

Rank	Name	Serving in ...	Coy/Platoon	Serving as ...
S/Sgt	Pearson	Glider Pilot Rgmt		Horsa Pilot
S/Sgt	Guthrie	Glider Pilot Rgmt		Horsa Co-Pilot
WO	Bain	RAF		Tug Pilot
Lt	Sweeney	2nd Oxf Bucks	D 23	Platoon Cdr
Sgt	Gooch	2nd Oxf Bucks	D 23	
Cpl	Murton	2nd Oxf Bucks	D 23	
Cpl	Howard	2nd Oxf Bucks	D 23	
Cpl	Jennings	2nd Oxf Bucks	D 23	
L/C	Porter	2nd Oxf Bucks	D 23	
Cpl	Stacey	2nd Oxf Bucks	D 23	
Pte	Allen	2nd Oxf Bucks	D 23	
Pte	Bowden	2nd Oxf Bucks	D 23	
Pte	Buller	2nd Oxf Bucks	D 23	
Pte	Bright	2nd Oxf Bucks	D 23	
Pte	Bleach	2nd Oxf Bucks	D 23	
Pte	Clark 46	2nd Oxf Bucks	D 23	
Pte	Galbraith	2nd Oxf Bucks	D 23	
Pte	Jackson 59	2nd Oxf Bucks	D 23	
Pte	Roach	2nd Oxf Bucks	D 23	
Pte	Roberts 94	2nd Oxf Bucks	D 23	
Pte	Read	2nd Oxf Bucks	D 23	
Pte	Tibbett	2nd Oxf Bucks	D 23	
Pte	Wixon	2nd Oxf Bucks	D 23	
Pte	Wood	2nd Oxf Bucks	D 23	
Pte	Willcocks	2nd Oxf Bucks	D 23	
Lt	Macdonald	7th Para		Liaison Officer
Cpl	Straw	Royal Engineers		
Spr	Bradford	Royal Engineers		
Spr	Carter	Royal Engineers		
Spr	Field	Royal Engineers		
Spr	Wilkinson	Royal Engineers		

Glider Number 5 landed in a field adjacent to the Orne River Bridge, not exactly where planned but very well positioned for the job that was to be done.

Glider Number 6 – Target, the Orne River Bridge.

Rank	Name	Serving in ...	Coy/Platoon	Serving as ...
S/Sgt	Howard	Glider Pilot Rgmt		Horsa Pilot
S/Sgt	Baacke	Glider Pilot Rgmt		Horsa Co-pilot
F/O	Archibald	RAF		Tug Pilot
Lt	Fox	2nd Oxf.Bucks	B 27	Platoon Cdr
Sgt	Thornton	2nd Oxf.Bucks	B 27	
Cpl	Lally	2nd Oxf.Bucks	B 27	
Cpl	Burns	2nd Oxf.Bucks	B 27	
L/C	Loveday	2nd Oxf.Bucks	B 27	
Pte	Collett	2nd Oxf.Bucks	B 27	
Pte	Hubbert	2nd Oxf.Bucks	B 27	
Pte	Clare	2nd Oxf.Bucks	B 27	
Pte	Peverill	2nd Oxf.Bucks	B 27	
Pte	Pope	2nd Oxf.Bucks	B 27	
Pte	Whitehouse	2nd Oxf.Bucks	B 27	
Pte	Whitbread	2nd Oxf.Bucks	B 27	
Pte	Lawton	2nd Oxf.Bucks	B 27	
Pte	Rudge	2nd Oxf.Bucks	B 27	
Pte	O'Shaughnessy	2nd Oxf.Bucks	B 27	
Pte	Annetts	2nd Oxf.Bucks	B 27	
Pte	Summersby	2nd Oxf.Bucks	B 27	
Pte	Woods	2nd Oxf.Bucks	B 27	
Pte	Wyatt	2nd Oxf.Bucks	B 27	
Pte	Ward	2nd Oxf.Bucks	B 27	
Pte	Storr	2nd Oxf.Bucks	B 27	
L/C	Lawson	RAMC		Medic
WS Lt	Bence	Royal Engineers		
Spr	Burns	Royal Engineers		
Spr	C.W.Larkin	Royal Engineers		
Spr	C.H.Larkin	Royal Engineers		
Spr	Maxted	Royal Engineers		

Glider Number 6 landed on schedule, close to the river bridge.

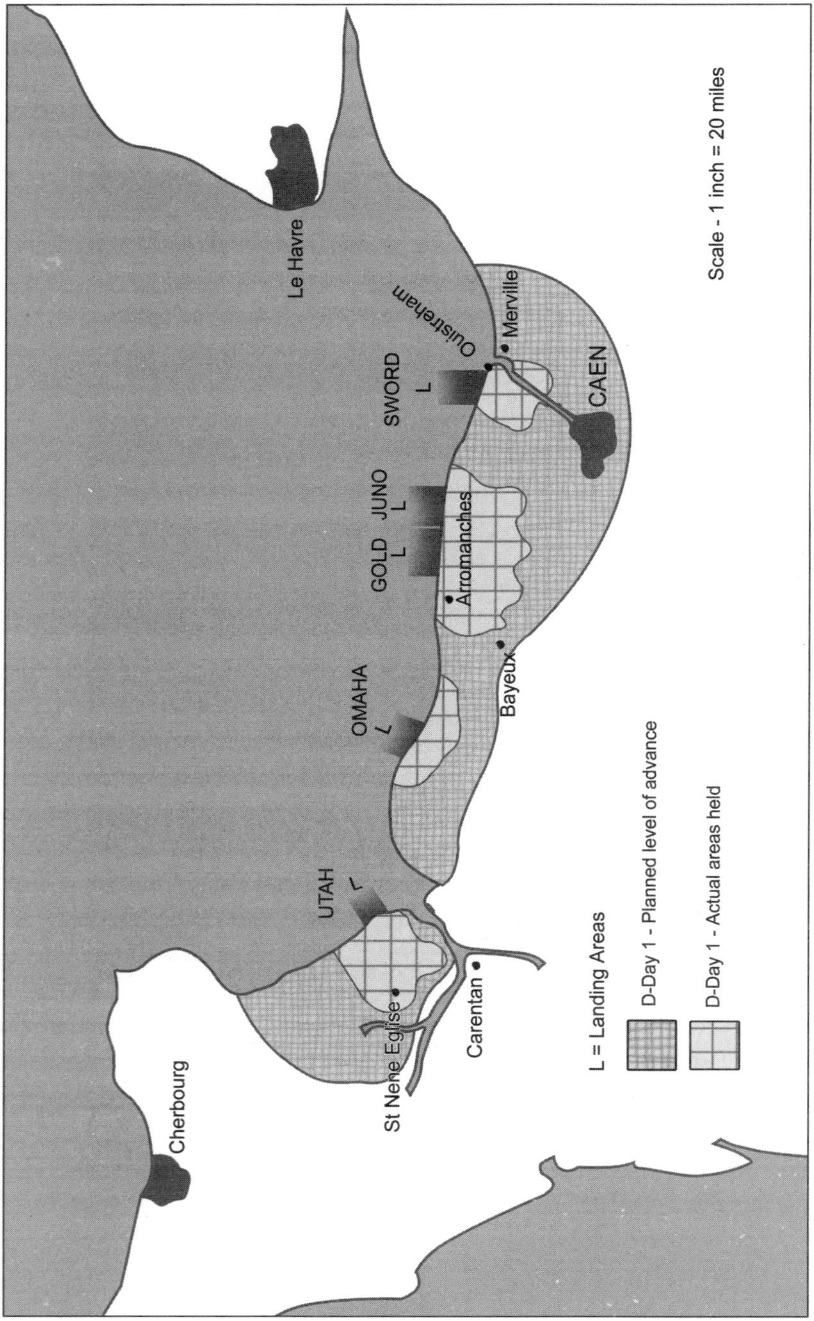
Le Havre
Ouistreham
Merville
SWORD
L
CAEN
JUNO
L
GOLD
L
Arromanches
Bayeux
OMAHA
L
UTAH
L
St Nene Eglise
Carentan
Cherbourg
L = Landing Areas
D-Day 1 - Planned level of advance
D-Day 1 - Actual areas held
Scale - 1 inch = 20 miles

Invasion Beaches

DIVISIONS THAT LANDED IN FRANCE ON 6TH JUNE. 1944 - D-DAY

OMAHA BEACH - 1st U.S. Division

116 Infantry   18 Infantry   26 Infantry
16 Infantry   115 Infantry   2nd Rangers
5th Rangers   741 Tank Bn   111 Field Artillery Bn
7 Field Artillery Bn   81 Chemical Bn

UTAH BEACH- 4th U.S. Division

8 Infantry   22 Infantry   12 Infantry
70 Tank Bn   359 Infantry (from 90th Division)

SWORD BEACH

3RD BRITISH DIVISION
8th Bde.
1st Bn. The Suffolk Regt.
2nd Bn. The East Yorkshire Regt.
1st Bn. The South Lancashire Regt.
9th Bde.
2nd Bn. The Lincolnshire Regt.
1st Bn. The King's Own Scottish Borderers
2nd Bn. The Royal Ulster Rifles
185th Bde.
2nd Bn. The Royal Warwickshire Regt.
1st Bn. The Royal Norfolk Regt.
2nd Bn. The King's Shropshire Light Infantry
27th Armoured Bde.
13th/18th Royal Hussars
1st East Riding Yeomanry
The Staffordshire Yeomanry

Divisional Troops
3rd Reconnaisance Regt. RAC
3rd Divisional Engineers
3rd Div. Signals
7th, 33rd and 76th Field, 20th Anti-Tank and 92nd Light Anti-Aircraft
Regts. RA
2nd Bn. The Middlesex Regt. (Machine Gun)

JUNO BEACH

3RD CANADIAN DIVISION.
7th Bde
The Royal Winnipeg Rifles
The Regina Rifle Regt.
The Canadian Scottish Regt.
8th Bde
The Queen's Own Rifles of Canada. The North Shore Regt
Le Regiment de la Chaudiere
9th Bde
The Highland Light Infantry of Canada. The Stormont,
Dundas and Glengarry Highlanders, The North Nova
Scotia Highlanders

Divisional Troops
7th Reconnaissance Regt (17th Duke of York's Royal Canadian
Hussars) 3rd Canadian Div Engineers.
3rd Canadian Div Signals. 12th, 13th, and 14th & 19th Field Regs, 3rd
Anti Tank and 4th Anti Aircraft Regts R.A.C.
The Cameron Highlanders of Ottawa (Machine Gun)
2nd Canadian Armoured Bde.
1st Hussars
The Fort Garry Horse
The Sherbrooke Fusiliers Regt.

GOLD BEACH

50TH BRITISH NORTHUMBRIAN DIVISION.
69th Bde
5th Bn The East Yorkshire Regt.
6th and 7th Bn   The Green Howards.
151st Bde
6th. 8th.and 9th. Bns The Durham Light Infantry
231st Bde
2nd Bt The Devonshire Regt.
1st Bt. The Hampshire Regt 1st Bt The Dorsetshire Regt.
42 Royal Marine Commando
56th Independent Bde.
2nd Bn South Wales Borderers.
 2nd Bn The Gloucestershire Regt. 2nd Bn The Essex regt.
8th Armoured Brigade
4/7th Royal Dragoon Guards
24th Lancers
The Sherwood Rangers Yeomanry

Divisional Troops
61st reconnaissance Regt. R.A.C. 50th Div. Engineers
 50th Div Signals 74th. 90th. And 124th Field, 102nd Anti-Tank
and 25th Light Anti- Aircraft Regts. R.A.
2nd Bn. The Cheshire Regt. (Machine Gun)

OTHER FORMATIONS.

30th Armoured Brigade. 22nd Dragoons. St Lothian and Border Horse and County of London Yeomanry (Westminster Dragoons)
141st Regt R.A.C.
1st Tank Brigade.   11th. 42nd and 49th Bns R.T.R.
1st Assault Brigade R.E. 5th. 6th.and 42nd Assault Regts. R.E..
79th Armoured Div. Signals
1st Canadian Armoured Personnel Carrier Regt.
1st Special Service Brigade   Nos 3,4, and 6 commandos
No 45 (Royal Marine) Commando.
4th Special Services Brigade. Nos 41. 46. 47 and 48 (Royal Marine) Commandos.
Armoured Support Group   1st and 2nd Royal Marine Armoured Support Regts.
Units of the Royal Artillery and Royal Engineers.

U.S. Airborne and Infantry Formantions

Squads 9 to 12 men
Three squads to a Platoon.
Four platoons to a Company.
Four Companies to a Battalion
Four Battalions to a Regiment.
Four Regiments to a Division.
Plus attached engineers, artillery, medical and other support personnel

British and Allied Army Formations
(Often Varied to suit situation)

Ten men to a section
Three Sections to a Platoon
Three Platoons to a Company
Four Companies to a Battalion
Three Battalions to a Brigade
Three Brigades to a Division
Three Divisions to a Corps
Three Corps to an Army